THE KEY TO THEOSOPHY
AN ABRIDGEMENT

When Helena Petrovna Blavatsky appeared on the American scene nearly one hundred years ago, she arrested attention through her display of extraordinary psychic powers. Of far greater importance, however, was her profound knowledge of metaphysical lore, including a familiarity with the religious and philosophical systems of the ancients, the mystery teachings of Egypt and Greece, the science of symbology and the higher aspects of occultism. From all these sources, guided by those she considered her spiritual teachers, she presented to the Western world the metaphysical system known as Theosophy. She was also one of the chief founders of The Theosophical Society, established in New York in 1875 and which has since spread to more than sixty countries throughout the world.

H. P. Blavatsky produced an immense body of literature, including *Isis Unveiled, The Secret Doctrine, The Voice of the Silence,* and numerous articles in the journals she had founded, *The Theosophist* and *Lucifer,* as well as in other periodicals. The publication of *The Key to Theosophy* in 1889 was hailed as the appearance of the first basic text on the subject, written as an introduction to the study of the theosophical philosophy and as a definition of the purposes for which The Theosophical Society had been established. The author herself characterized the nature of the work in her sub-title, "A clear exposition in the form of Question and Answer of the Ethics, Science and Philosophy, for the Study of which the Theosophical Society has been founded." The book has been through several editions and numerous printings and has remained a classic for all students of Theosophy. Because of the increasing interest in the subject the work is presented now in paperbound abridged edition.

Also available in Quest paperbound editions are *An Abridgement of The Secret Doctrine* and *The Voice of the Silence.*

THE

KEY TO THEOSOPHY

by

H. P. BLAVATSKY

AN ABRIDGEMENT

edited by

Joy Mills

A QUEST BOOK

THE THEOSOPHICAL PUBLISHING HOUSE
Wheaton, Ill., U.S.A.
Madras, India / London, England

© Copyright The Theosophical Publishing House 1972

The Theosophical Publishing House is a department of The Theosophical Society in America, Wheaton, Illinois

Original complete edition 1889

Abridged Quest edition 1972

Library of Congress Catalog Card Number 75-181716

ISBN: 0-8356-0427-6

Manufactured in the United States of America

Dedicated

by

"H. P. B."

To all her Pupils,

that

They may Learn and Teach

in their turn.

CONTENTS

SECTION I

THEOSOPHY AND THE THEOSOPHICAL SOCIETY:

SECTION II

EXOTERIC AND ESOTERIC THEOSOPHY:

SECTION III

THE WORKING SYSTEM OF THE T. S.:

INTRODUCTION

With the establishment of The Theosophical Society in New York City in 1875, the terms *Theosophy* and *Theosophical* were introduced into the vocabulary of 19th century western culture. During the formative years of the Society's existence, however, little attempt was made either to define these terms or to clarify their specific meaning. The earliest presentations, both written and spoken, by those who were the Society's principal founders, H. P. Blavatsky and H. S. Olcott, focused on the reintroduction into world thought of an ageless wisdom whose golden thread could be traced through successive cultures, civilizations and epochs. Blavatsky's own initial work, *Isis Unveiled,* published just two years after the Society's founding, was a voluminous compendium of philosophical, religious, scientific, mythological, allegorical, and symbolical facts and theories, pointing to the immense antiquity of the occult tradition. Her magnum opus, *The Secret Doctrine,* published in 1888, was a comprehensive presentation of the essential teachings of the esoteric philosophy on both Cosmogenesis and Anthropogenesis, the origins and workings of universal laws in both nature and man.

The appearance of *The Key to Theosophy* in 1889, one of the last two books by H. P. Blavatsky to be published in her lifetime (the other being *The Voice of the Silence,* a work consisting of excerpts which she translated from "The Book of Golden Precepts," a mystical treatise in the tradition of Mahayana Buddhism), gave both The Theosophical Society and the world at large a basic text outlining what one early reviewer of the work called "the anatomy and physiology of Theosophy."* H.B.P. (as she was known) was

---

* The publication of *Esoteric Buddhism* by A. P. Sinnett, an early member and leading figure in The Theosophical Society following the moving of the founders to India, must be considered technically as the first descriptive exposition of the theosophical philosophy *per se.* Appearing in 1883, this work brought together teachings and information conveyed to Mr. Sinnett through a most remarkable correspondence known as the "Mahatma Letters." Unfortunately, however, the title of Mr. Sinnett's work led many to believe that Theosophy was merely a new form of the religion known as Buddhism, a misunderstanding dealt with at length by H. P. Blavatsky in *The Key to Theosophy.*

undoubtedly aware of the need for just such a simple, yet comprehensive, presentation which would serve both to clarify the teachings sponsored by The Theosophical Society* and to correct the numerous misconceptions which had arisen concerning the Society's work and the theosophical philosophy. Since she was herself largely responsible for the introduction of that philosophy into Western thought and since she consistently maintained that she was but the spokesman for Eastern adept personages whom she considered her teachers, she was in the unenviable position of knowing better than anyone else the extent of the misconceptions which had arisen in connection with the theosophical philosophy. Certainly no one knew better than she did the vituperative abuse heaped upon the young Society she had co-founded, for the greater portion of that abuse was directed against her.

The issuance of *The Key to Theosophy* marked the first time since the Society's founding that the term "Theosophy" had been used in the title of a book. The nature of the work itself, and by implication its aim, was described by the sub-title, "A clear exposition, in the form of Questions and Answers, of the Ethics, Science and Philosophy for the study of which the Theosophical Society has been founded." The format adopted by the author was particularly appropriate in meeting the needs that must have existed at the time, for the mythical questioner posed the very inquiries on which so many of the attacks against and the misconceptions about Theosophy and the Society's purposes were based.

H.P.B., then resident in London, had about her a group of close associates who, as pupils aware of the tremendous knowledge and unique capacity of their teacher, were plying

---

* The term sponsorship should not be taken to indicate that the Society imposes either dogma or belief on any of its members. Rather, as has been suggested by many, the name of the Society itself implies an objective not expressly stated in the Three Objects officially designated by the organization, namely the presentation of a philosophy known as Theosophy. It is this presentation that may be said to be sponsored by the Society, while at the same time the Society maintains a platform of full freedom of thought for all who pursue the study or who join its ranks. Consequently, as H.P.B. herself emphasized in *The Key*, the Society is both non-dogmatic and non-sectarian; "it was formed to assist in showing to men that such a thing as Theosophy exists, and to help them in ascending towards it by studying and assimilating its eternal verities."

her with numerous questions concerning the Wisdom-Religion, as Theosophy was frequently called. Consequently, she knew at first hand the need that existed among theosophical students for a systematic exposition of the philosophy. Therefore, her book answered not only the critics of the Society, but also provided sympathetic students with a clear, concise, readily comprehensible exposition of the fundamental principles of Theosophy itself. The book remains today, as it was on the day of its first publication, the classic response both to those who would understand the "Religio-Philosophico-Cosmico-Ethical" system which is Theosophy and to those who would distort the truth of that system or vilify the Society which serves as the channel for its expression. Nowhere, before or since, has the Society's singular purpose been so clearly or so effectively stated. Nowhere has the Society's task and its possible future been so ably and so inspiringly delineated.

Why, then, an abridgement, if the book "teaches the anatomy and physiology of Theosophy"? Quite simply, because much that is contained in the original draws inevitably upon references and views current in H.P.B.'s day, and the inquirer who wishes to come quickly to the "bare bones" of Theosophy may feel frustrated in his search by the numerous passages that only cloak the "anatomy." An effort has been made, therefore, to strip away the less essential, including references no longer pertinent, quotations whose relevancy has disappeared with the passage of time, and arguments that have little if any meaning for the modern reader. The *Abridgement,* is based upon the original 1889 edition, the full text of which is readily available in print; there have been no textual alterations, no editorial interpolations, and no interpretative commentaries. One or two editorial footnotes, clearly designated as such, have been added to clarify certain terms which, today, have taken on meanings far removed from the usage of the last century. The sole purpose in preparing the *Abridgement* has been to make readily and easily available the fundamental teachings of Theosophy as presented by its most remarkable exponent, H. P. Blavatsky, while at the same time preserving the flavor, the vigor and the vital quality of the original work.

A key is meant for unlocking doors. For countless thousands, Theosophy has been the key that has opened doors of the mind and heart inward upon magnificent vistas of wisdom and understanding. It has been the key to the treasures of the illumined spirit, the treasures of love and compassion that, shared, form the Supreme Treasure, Brotherhood Universal. To be given such a key is not enough, however; to unlock the secrets of knowledge, to open the doors of perception, to release the jewels of compassion, one must turn the key. If this *Abridgement* of a timeless classic, *The Key to Theosophy*, encourages yet other students to try the doors that lead toward wisdom, to put knowledge to work in the service of humanity, it will have fulfilled a useful role.

—JOY MILLS

PREFACE

THE purpose of this book is exactly expressed in its title, "THE KEY TO THEOSOPHY," and needs but few words of explanation. It is not a complete or exhaustive text-book of Theosophy, but only a key to unlock the door that leads to the deeper study. It traces the broad outlines of the Wisdom Religion, and explains its fundamental principles; meeting, at the same time, the various objections raised by the average Western enquirer, and endeavouring to present unfamiliar concepts in a form as simple and in language as clear as possible. That it should succeed in making Theosophy intelligible without mental effort on the part of the reader would be too much to expect; but it is hoped that the obscurity still left is of the thought not of the language, is due to depth not to confusion. To the mentally lazy or obtuse, Theosophy must remain a riddle; for in the world mental as in the world spiritual each man must progress by his own efforts. The writer cannot do the reader's thinking for him, nor would the latter be any the better off if such vicarious thought were possible.

Very hearty thanks are due from the author to many Theosophists who have sent suggestions and questions, or have otherwise contributed help during the writing of this book. The work will be the more useful for their aid, and that will be their best reward.

H. P. B.

I

THEOSOPHY AND THE THEOSOPHICAL SOCIETY

THE MEANING OF THE NAME

ENQUIRER. Theosophy and its doctrines are often referred to as a newfangled religion. Is it a religion?

THEOSOPHIST. It is not. Theosophy is Divine Knowledge or Science.

ENQ. What is the real meaning of the term?

THEO. "Divine Wisdom," θεοσοφία (Theosophia) or Wisdom of the gods, as θεογονία (theogonia), genealogy of the gods. The word θεός means a god in Greek, one of the divine beings, certainly not "God" in the sense attached in our day to the term. Therefore, it is not "Wisdom of God," as translated by some, but *Divine Wisdom* such as that possessed by the gods.

ENQ. What is the origin of the name?

THEO. It comes to us from the Alexandrian philosophers, called lovers of truth, Philaletheians, from φιλ (phil) "loving," and ἀλήθεια (aletheia) "truth." The name Theosophy dates from the third century of our era, and began with Ammonius Saccas and his disciples,"*

---

*Also called Analogeticists. As explained by Prof. Alex Wilder, F.T.S., [Fellow, The Theosophical Society] in his *New Platonism and Alchemy: The Eclectic Philosophy*, they were called so because of their practice of interpreting all sacred legends and narratives, myths and mysteries, by a rule or principle of analogy and correspondence: so that events which were related as having occurred in the external world were regarded as expressing operations and experiences of the human soul. They were also denominated Neo-Platonists. Though Theosophy, or the Eclectic Theosophical system, is generally attributed to the third century, yet, if Diogenes Laertius is to be credited, its origin is much earlier, as he attributed the system to an Egyptian priest, Pot-Amun, who lived in the early days of the Ptolemaic dynasty. The same author tells us that the name is Coptic, and signifies one consecrated to Amun, the God of Wisdom. Theosophy is the equivalent of Brahmā-Vidya, divine knowledge.

who started the Eclectic Theosophical system.

ENQ. What was the object of this system?

THEO. First of all to inculcate certain great moral truths
    upon its disciples, and all those who were "lovers of
    the truth." Hence the motto adopted by the Theo-
    sophical Society: "There is no religion higher than
    truth."* The chief aim of the Founders of the Eclectic
    Theosophical School was one of the three objects of its
    modern successor, the Theosophical Society, namely, to
    reconcile all religions, sects and nations under a com-
    mon system of ethics, based on eternal verities.

ENQ. What have you to show that this is not an impossible
    dream; and that all the world's religions *are* based on
    the one and the same truth?

THEO. Their comparative study and analysis. "All the old
    worships indicate the existence of a single theosophy
    anterior to them. 'The key that is to open one must
    open all; otherwise it cannot be the right key.' "†

THE POLICY OF THE THEOSOPHICAL SOCIETY

ENQ. In the days of Ammonius there were several ancient
    great religions, and numerous were the sects in Egypt
    and Palestine alone. How could he reconcile them?

---

*Eclectic Theosophy was divided under three heads: (1) Belief in one abso-
    lute, incomprehensible and supreme Deity, or infinite essence, which is
    the root of all nature, and of all that is, visible and invisible. (2) Belief
    in man's eternal immortal nature, because, being a radiation of the
    Universal Soul, it is of an identical essence with it. (3) *Theurgy,* or
    "divine work," or *producing a work of gods;* from *theoi,* "gods," and
    ergein "to work." The term is very old, but, as it belongs to the voca-
    bulary of the MYSTERIES, was not in popular use. It was a mystic be-
    lief — practically proven by initiated adepts and priests — that, by
    making oneself as pure as the incorporeal beings — *i.e.,* by returning
    to one's pristine purity of nature — man could move the gods to im-
    part to him Divine mysteries, and even cause them to become occa-
    sionally visible, either subjectively or objectively.

†Wilder, *op. cit.,* p. 11.

THEO. By doing that which we again try to do now. The Neo-Platonists were a large body, and belonged to various religious philosophies; so do our Theosophists. In those days, the Jew Aristobulus affirmed that the ethics of Aristotle represented the *esoteric* teachings of the Law of Moses; Philo Judaeus endeavoured to reconcile the *Pentateuch* with the Pythagorean and Platonic philosophy; and Josephus proved that the Essenes of Carmel were simply the copyists and followers of the Egyptian Therapeutae (the healers). So it is in our day. We can show the line of descent of every Christian religion, as of every, even the smallest, sect. The latter are the minor twigs or shoots grown on the larger branches; but shoots and branches spring from the same trunk — the WISDOM-RELIGION. To prove this was the aim of Ammonius, who endeavoured to induce Gentiles and Christians, Jews and Idolaters, to lay aside their contentions and strifes, remembering only that they were all in possession of the same truth under various vestments, and were all the children of a common mother. This is the aim of Theosophy likewise.

ENQ. What are your authorities for saying this of the ancient Theosophists of Alexandria?

THEO. An almost countless number of well-known writers. Mosheim, one of them, says that:

Ammonius taught that the religion of the multitude went hand-in-hand with philosophy, and with her had shared the fate of being by degrees corrupted and obscured with mere human conceits, superstition, and lies; that it ought, therefore, to be brought back to its original purity by purging it of this dross and expounding it upon philosophical principles; and that the whole which Christ had in view was to reinstate and restore to its primitive integrity the Wisdom of the ancients — to reduce within bounds the universally-prevailing dominion of superstition — and in part to correct, and in part to exterminate the various errors that had found their way into the different popular religions.*

---

*Wilder, *op. cit.,* p. 5.

This, again, is precisely what the modern Theosophists say. Only while the great Philaletheian was supported and helped in the policy he pursued by two Church Fathers, Clement and Athenagoras, by all the learned Rabbis of the Synagogue, the Academy and the Groves, and while he taught a common doctrine for all, we, his followers on the same line, receive no recognition, but, on the contrary, are abused and persecuted. People 1,500 years ago are thus shown to have been more tolerant than they are in this *enlightened* century.

ENQ. Was he encouraged and supported by the Church because, notwithstanding his heresies, Ammonius taught Christianity and was a Christian?

THEO. Not at all. He was born a Christian, but never accepted Church Christianity. As said of him by the same writer:

> He had but to propound his instructions "according to the ancient pillars of Hermes, which Plato and Pythagoras knew before, and from them constituted their philosophy." Finding the same sentiments in the prologue of the Gospel according to St. John, he very properly supposed that the purpose of Jesus was to restore the great doctrine of Wisdom in its primitive integrity. The narratives of the Bible and the stories of the gods, he considered to be allegories illustrative of the truth, or else fables to be rejected."*

THE WISDOM-RELIGION ESOTERIC IN ALL AGES

ENQ. Since Ammonius never commited anything to writing, how can one feel sure that such were his teachings?

THEO. Neither did Buddha, Pythagoras, Confucius, Orpheus, Socrates, or even Jesus, leave behind them any writings. Yet most of these are historical personages, and their teachings have all survived. The disciples of Ammonius (among whom Origen and Herennios) wrote treatises and explained his ethics. Moreover, his pupils

---

*Wilder, *op. cit.*, pp. 8-9, 5.

— Origen, Plotinus, and Longinus (counsellor of the famous Queen Zenobia) — have all left voluminous records of the Philaletheian System — so far, at all events, as their public profession of faith was known, for the school was divided into exoteric and *esoteric* teachings.

ENQ. How have the latter tenets reached our day, since you hold that what is properly called the WISDOM-RELIGION was esoteric?

THEO. The WISDOM-RELIGION was ever one, and being the last word of possible human knowledge, was, therefore, carefully preserved. It preceded by long ages the Alexandrian Theosophists, reached the modern, and will survive every other religion and philosophy.

ENQ. Where and by whom was it so preserved? ·

THEO. Among Initiates of every country; among profound seekers after truth — their disciples; and in those parts of the world where such topics have always been most valued and pursued: in India, Central Asia, and Persia.

ENQ. Can you give me some proofs of its esotericism?

THEO. The best proof you can have of the fact is that every ancient religious, or rather philosophical, cult consisted of an esoteric or secret teaching, and an exoteric (outward public) worship. Furthermore, it is a well-known fact that the MYSTERIES of the ancients comprised with every nation the "greater" (secret) and "Lesser" (public) MYSTERIES — *e.g.*, in the celebrated solemnities called the *Eleusinia*, in Greece. From the Hierophants of Samothrace, Egypt, and the initiated Brahmins of the India of old, down to the later Hebrew Rabbis, all preserved, for fear of profanation, their real *bona fide* beliefs secret. The Jewish Rabbis called their secular religious series the *Merkabah* (the exterior body), "the vehicle," or, *the covering which contains the hidden soul — i.e.*, their highest secret knowledge. Not one of the ancient nations ever imparted through its priests its real philosophical secrets to the masses, but allotted to the latter only the husks. Northern Buddhism has its "greater" and its "lesser" vehicle, known as the *Mahayana* and the *Hinayana* Schools. Pythagoras called his *Gnosis* "the knowledge of things that are," and preserved that knowledge for his pledged disciples only: for those who could digest such mental food and feel satisfied; and he pledged them to silence and secrecy. Occult alphabets and secret ciphers are the development of the old Egyptian *hieratic* writings, the secret of which was, in the days of old, in the possession only of the Hierogrammatists, or initiated Egyptian priests. Ammonius Saccas, as his biographers tell us, bound his pupils by oath not to divulge *his higher doctrines* except to those who had already been instructed in preliminary knowledge, and who were also bound by a pledge. Finally, do we not find the same even in early Christianity, among the Gnostics, and even in the teachings of Christ? Did he not speak to the multitudes in parables which had a twofold meaning, and explain his reasons only to his disciples? "Unto you," he says, "it is given to know the mystery of the kingdom of God; but unto them that are without, all these things are done in parables" (*Mark,* iv, 11). "The Essenes of Judea and Carmel made similar distinctions, dividing their adherents into neophytes, brethren and the *perfect,*" or those initiated.* Examples might be brought from every country to this effect.

ENQ. Can you attain the "Secret Wisdom" simply by study?

THEO. I think not. Ancient Theosophists claimed, and so do the modern, that the infinite cannot be known by the finite — *i.e.,* sensed by the finite Self — but that the divine essence could be communicated to the higher spiritual Self in a state of ecstasy.

ENQ. What is your explanation of it?

THEO. Real ecstasy was defined by Plotinus as "the liberation of the mind from its finite consciousness, becoming

---

*Wilder, *op. cit.,* p. 7.

one and identified with the infinite." It is identical with that state which is known in India as *Samadhi*. The latter is practised by the Yogis, who facilitate it physically by the greatest abstinence in food and drink, and mentally by an incessant endeavour to purify and elevate the mind. Meditation is silent and unuttered prayer, or, as Plato expressed it, "the ardent turning of the soul toward the divine; not to ask any particular good (as in the common meaning of prayer), but for good itself — for the universal Supreme Good" of which we are a part on earth, and out of the essence of which we have all emerged. Therefore, adds Plato, "remain silent in the presence of the *divine ones,* till they remove the clouds from thy eyes and enable thee to see by the light which issues from themselves, not what appears as good to thee, but what is intrinsically good."*

ENQ. Theosophy, then, is not, as held by some, a newly devised scheme?

THEO. Only ignorant people can thus refer to it. It is as old as the world, in its teachings and ethics, if not in name, as it is also the broadest and most catholic system among all.

ENQ. How comes it, then, that Theosophy has remained so unknown to the nations of the Western Hemisphere? Why should it have been a sealed book to races confessedly the most cultured and advanced?

THEO. We believe there were nations as cultured in days of old and certainly more spiritually "advanced" than we are. But there are several reasons for this willing ignorance. One of them was given by St. Paul to the cultured Athenians — a loss, for long centuries, of real

---

*Real Theosophy is, for the mystics, that state which Apollonius of Tyana was made to describe thus: "I can see the present and the future as in a clear mirror. The sage need not wait for the vapours of the earth and the corruption of the air to foresee plagues and fevers. . . . The *theoi* or gods see the future; common men, the present; sages, that which is about to take place." "The Theosophy of the Sages" he speaks of is well expressed in the assertion, "The Kingdom of God is within us."

spiritual insight, and even interest, owing to their too great devotion to things of sense and their long slavery to the dead letter of dogma and ritualism. But the strongest reason for it lies in the fact that real Theosophy has ever been kept secret.

ENQ. You have brought forward proofs that such secrecy has existed; but what was the real cause for it?

THEO. The causes for it were: *First,* the perversity of average human nature and its selfishness, always tending to the gratification of *personal* desires to the detriment of neighbours and next of kin. Such people could never be entrusted with *divine* secrets. *Secondly,* their unreliability to keep the sacred and divine knowledge from desecration. It is the latter that led to the perversion of the most sublime truths and symbols, and to the gradual transformation of things spiritual into anthropomorphic, concrete, and gross imagery — in other words, to the dwarfing of the god-idea and to idolatry.

THEOSOPHY IS NOT BUDDHISM

ENQ. You are often spoken of as "Esoteric Buddhists." Are you then all followers of Gautama Buddha?

THEO. No more than musicians are all followers of Wagner. Some of us are Buddhists by religion; yet there are far more Hindus and Brahmins than Buddhists among us, and more Christian-born Europeans and Americans than *converted* Buddhists. The mistake has arisen from a misunderstanding of the real meaning of the title of Mr. Sinnett's excellent work, *Esoteric Buddhism,* which last word ought to have been spelt *with one, instead of two, d's,* as then *Budhism* would have meant what it was intended for, merely "Wisdom*ism*" (Bodha, bodhi, "intelligence," "wisdom") instead of *Buddhism,* Gautama's religious philosophy. Theosophy, as already said, is the WISDOM-RELIGION.

ENQ. What is the difference between Buddhism, the religion founded by the Prince of Kapilavastu, and *Budhism,* the "Wisdomism" which you say is synonymous with Theosophy?

THEO. Just the same difference as there is between the secret teachings of Christ, which are called "the mysteries of the Kingdom of Heaven," and the later ritualism and dogmatic theology of the Churches and Sects. *Buddha* means the "Enlightened" by *Bodha,* or understanding, Wisdom. This has passed root and branch into the *esoteric* teachings that Gautama imparted to his chosen *Arhats* only.

ENQ. But some Orientalists deny that Buddha ever taught any esoteric doctrine at all?

THEO. They may as well deny that Nature has any hidden secrets for the men of science. Farther on I will prove it by Buddha's conversation with his disciple Ananda. His esoteric teachings were simply the *Gupta-Vidya* (secret knowledge) of the ancient Brahmins, the key to which their modern successors have, with few exceptions, completely lost. And this *Vidya* has passed into what is now known as the *inner* teachings of the *Mahayana* school of Northern Buddhism. Those who deny it are simply ignorant pretenders to Orientalism.

ENQ. But are not the ethics of Theosophy identical with those taught by Buddha?

THEO. Certainly, because these ethics are the soul of the Wisdom-Religion, and were once the common property of the initiates of all nations. But Buddha was the first to embody these lofty ethics in his public teachings, and to make them the foundation and the very essence of his public system. It is herein that lies the immense difference between exoteric Buddhism and every other religion. For while in other religions ritualism and dogma hold the first and most important place, in Buddhism it is the ethics which have always been the most insisted upon. This accounts for the resemblance, amounting almost to identity, between the ethics of Theosophy and those of the religion of Buddha.

ENQ. Are there any great points of difference?

THEO. One great distinction between Theosophy and *exoteric* Buddhism is that the latter entirely denies (*a*) the existence of any Deity, and (*b*) any conscious *post-mortem* life, or even any self-conscious surviving individuality in man. And it is so, if we refer only to Buddha's public teachings; the reason for such reticence on his part I will give farther on. But the schools of the Northern Buddhist Church, established in those countries to which his initiated Arhats retired after the Master's death, teach all that is now called Theosophical doctrines, because they form part of the knowledge of the initiates. Yet Theosophy is not Buddhism.

II

EXOTERIC AND ESOTERIC THEOSOPHY

WHAT THE MODERN THEOSOPHICAL SOCIETY IS NOT

ENQ. Your doctrines, then, are not a revival of Buddhism, nor are they entirely copied from the Neo-Platonic Theosophy?

THEO. They are not. But to these questions I cannot give you a better answer than by quoting from a paper read on "Theosophy" by Dr. J. D. Buck, F.T.S., before the Theosophical Convention, at Chicago, America (April, 1889).

The Theosophical Society was organized for the purpose of promulgating the Theosophical doctrines, and for the promotion of the Theosophic life. The present Theosophical Society is not the first of its kind. I have a volume entitled: "Theosophical Transactions of the Philadelphian Society," published in London in 1697; and another with the following title: "Introduction to Theosophy, or the Science of the Mystery of Christ; that is, of Deity, Nature, and Creature, embracing the philosophy of all the working powers of life, magical and spiritual, and forming a practical guide to the sublimest purity, sanctity, and evangelical perfection; also the attainment of divine vision, and the holy angelic arts, potencies, and other prerogatives of the regeneration," published in London in 1855.

In the following year (1856) another volume was issued, royal octavo, of 600 pages, diamond type, of "Theosophical Miscellanies." Of the last-named work 500 copies only were issued, for gratuitous distribution to Libraries and Universities. These earlier movements, of which there were many, originated within the Church, with persons of great piety and earnestness, and of unblemished character; and all of these writings were in orthodox form, using the Christian expressions, and, like the writings of the eminent Churchman William Law, would only be distinguished by the ordinary reader for their great earnestness and piety. These were one and all but attempts to derive and explain the deeper meanings and original import of the Christian Scriptures, and to illustrate and unfold the Theosophic life. At the time of the Reformation John Reuchlin made a similar attempt with the same result, though he was the intimate and trusted friend of Luther. Orthodoxy never desired to be informed and enlightened. These reformers were informed, as was Paul by Festus, that too much learning had made them mad, and that it would be dangerous to go farther. Passing by the verbiage, which was partly a matter of habit and education with these writers, and partly due to religious restraint through secular power, and coming to the core of the matter, these writings were Theosophical in the strictest sense, and pertain solely to man's knowledge of his own nature and the higher life of the soul. The present Theosophical movement has sometimes been declared to be an attempt to convert Christendom to Buddhism, which means simply that the word "Heresy" has lost its terrors and relinquished its power. Individuals in every age have more or less clearly apprehended the Theosophical doctrines and wrought them into the fabric of their lives. These doctrines belong exclusively to no religion, and are confined to no society or time. They are the birthright of every human soul. Such a thing as orthodoxy must be wrought out by each individual according to his nature and his needs, and according to his varying experience. This may explain why those who have imagined Theosophy to be a new religion have hunted in vain for its creed and its ritual. Its creed is Loyalty to Truth, and its ritual "To honour every truth by use."

How little this principle of Universal Brotherhood is understood by the masses of mankind, how seldom its transcendent importance is recognized, may be seen in the diversity of opinion and fictitious interpretations regarding the Theosophical Society. This Society was organized on this one principle, the essential Brotherhood of Man. It has been assailed as Buddhistic and anti-Christian, as though it could be both these together, when both Buddhism and Christianity, as set forth by their inspired founders, make brotherhood the one essential of doctrine and of life. Theosophy has been also regarded as something new under the sun, or at best as old mysticism masquerading under a new name. While it is true that many Societies founded upon, and united to support, the principles of altruism, or essential brotherhood, have borne various names, it is also true that many have also been called Theosophic, and with principles and aims as the present society bearing that name.

No better or more explicit answer could be given to your questions.

ENQ. Which system do you prefer or follow, in that case, besides Buddhistic ethics?

THEO. None, and all. We hold to no religion, as to no philosophy in particular: we cull the good we find in each. But here, again, it must be stated that, like all other ancient systems, Theosophy is divided into Exoteric and *Esoteric Sections.*

ENQ. What is the difference?

THEO. The members of the Theosophical Society at large are free to profess whatever religion or philosophy they like, or none if they so prefer, provided they are in sympathy with, and ready to carry out one or more of the three objects of the Association. The Society is a philanthropic and scientific body for the propagation of the idea of brotherhood on *practical* instead of *theoretical* lines. The Fellows may be Christians or Mussulmans, Jews or Parsees, Buddhists or Brahmins, Spiritualists or Materialists, it does not matter; but every member must be either a philanthropist, or a scholar. In short, he has to help, if he can, in the carrying out of at least one of the objects of the programme. Otherwise he has no reason for becoming a "Fellow." Such are the majority of the exoteric Society, composed of "attached" and "unattached" members.* These may,

---

* An "attached member" means one who has joined some particular branch of the T. S. An "unattached," one who belongs to the Society at large, has his diploma, from the Headquarters (Adyar, Madras), but is connected with no branch or lodge.

or may not, become Theosophists *de facto*. Members they are, by virtue of their having joined the Society; but the latter cannot make a Theosophist of one who has no sense for the *divine* fitness of things, or of him who understands Theosophy in his own — if the expression may be used — *sectarian* and egotistic way.

THEOSOPHISTS AND MEMBERS OF THE T.S.

ENQ. What of those who pursue the esoteric study of Theosophy; are they the real Theosophists?

THEO. Not necessarily, until they have proven themselves to be such. They have entered the inner group and pledged themselves to carry out, as strictly as they can, the rules of the occult body. This is a difficult undertaking, as the foremost rule of all is the entire renunciation of one's personality. The few real Theosophists in the T. S. are among these members. This does not imply that outside of the T. S. there are no Theosophists; for there are, and more than people know of.

ENQ. Then what is the good of joining the so-called Theosophical Society in that case? Where is the incentive?

THEO. None, except the advantage of deriving much help from mutual aid and sympathy. Union is strength and harmony, and well-regulated simultaneous efforts produce wonders. This has been the secret of all associations and communities since mankind existed.

ENQ. But why could not a man of well-balanced mind and singleness of purpose, one, say, of indomitable energy and perseverance, become an Occultist and even an Adept if he works alone?

THEO. He may; but there are ten thousand chances against one that he will fail. For one reason out of many others, no books on Occultism or Theurgy exist in our day which give out the secrets of alchemy or mediaeval

Theosophy in plain language. All are symbolical or in parables; and as the key to these has been lost for ages in the West, how can a man learn the correct meaning of what he is reading and studying? Therein lies the greatest danger, one that leads to unconscious *black** magic or the most helpless mediumship. He who has not an Initiate for a master had better leave the dangerous study alone. Look around you and observe. While two-thirds of *civilized* society ridicule the mere notion that there is anything in Theosophy, Occultism, Spiritualism, or in the Kabala, the other third is composed of the most heterogeneous and opposite elements. Some believe in the mystical, and even in the *supernatural* (!), but each believes in his own way. Result: no two men think alike, no two are agreed upon any fundamental occult principles, though many are those who claim for themselves the *ultima Thule* of knowledge, and would make outsiders believe that they are full-blown adepts. Not only is there no scientific and accurate knowledge of Occultism accessible in the West — not even of true astrology, the only branch of Occultism which, in its *exoteric* teachings, has definite laws and a definite system — but no one has any idea of what real Occultism means. Some limit ancient wisdom to the *Kabala* and the Jewish *Zohar,* which each interprets in his own way according to the dead-letter of the Rabbinical methods. Others regard Swedenborg or Boehme as the ultimate expressions of the highest wisdom; while others again see in mesmerism the great secret of ancient magic. One and all of those who put their theory into practice are rapidly drifting, through ignorance, into black magic. Happy are those who escape from it, as they have neither test nor criterion by which they can distinguish between the true and the false.

A tree is known by its fruit, a system by its results. When our opponents are able to prove to us that any solitary student of Occultism throughout the ages has

---

*[The use of this term is in no way related to skin color. — Ed.]

become a saintly adept like Ammonius Saccas, or even a Plotinus, or a Theurgist like Iamblichus, or achieved feats such as are claimed to have been done by Saint-Germain, without any master to guide him, and all this without being a medium, a self-deluded psychic, or a charlatan — then shall we confess ourselves mistaken. But till then, Theosophists prefer to follow the proven natural law of the tradition of the Sacred Science. There are mystics who have made great discoveries in chemistry and physical sciences, almost bordering on alchemy and Occultism; others who, by the sole aid of their genius, have rediscovered portions, if not the whole, of the lost alphabets of the "Mystery language," and are, therefore, able to read correctly Hebrew scrolls; others still, who, being seers, have caught wonderful *glimpses* of the hidden secrets of Nature. But all these are *specialists*. One is a theoretical inventor, another a Hebrew, *i.e.,* a Sectarian Kabalist, a third a Swedenborg of modern times, denying all and everything outside of his own particular science or religion. Not one of them can boast of having produced a universal or even a national benefit thereby, not even to himself. With the exception of a few healers none have helped with their science Humanity, nor even a number of men of the same community. Where are the Chaldees of old, those who wrought marvellous cures, "not by charms but by simples"? Where is an Appollonius of Tyana, who healed the sick and raised the dead under any climate and circumstances?

Enq. Is the production of such healing adepts the aim of Theosophy?

Theo. Its aims are several; but the most important of all are those which are likely to lead to the relief of human suffering under any or every form, moral as well as physical. And we believe the former to be far more important than the latter. Theosophy has to inculcate ethics; it has to purify the soul if it would relieve the physical body, whose ailments, save cases of accidents, are all hereditary. It is not by studying Occultism for selfish ends, for the gratification of one's personal ambition, pride, or vanity, that one can ever reach the true goal: that of helping suffering mankind. Nor is it by studying one single branch of the esoteric philosophy that a man becomes an Occultist, but by studying, if not mastering, them all.

THE DIFFERENCE BETWEEN THEOSOPHY AND OCCULTISM

ENQ. You speak of Theosophy and Occultism; are they identical?

THEO. By no means. A man may be a very good Theosophist indeed, whether *in* or *outside* of the Society, without being in any way an Occultist. But no one can be a true Occultist without being a real Theosophist; otherwise he is simply a black magician, whether conscious or unconscious.

ENQ. What do you mean?

THEO. I have said already that a true Theosophist must put in practice the loftiest moral ideal, must strive to realize his unity with the whole of humanity, and work ceaselessly for others. Now, if an Occultist does not do all this, he must act selfishly for his own personal benefit; and if he has acquired more practical power than other ordinary men, he becomes forthwith a far more dangerous enemy to the world and those around him than the average mortal.

ENQ. Then is an Occultist simply a man who possesses more power than other people?

THEO. Far more — if he is a *practical* and really learned Occultist, and not one only in name. Occult sciences are *not,* as described in Encyclopaedias, "those *imaginary* sciences of the Middle Ages which related to the *supposed* action or influence of Occult qualities or supernatural powers, as alchemy, magic, necromancy, and astrology," for they are real, actual, and very dangerous sciences. They teach the secret potency of things in Nature, developing and cultivating the hidden powers "latent in man," thus giving him tremendous advantages over more ignorant mortals.

ENQ. But are not all these Occult sciences, magic, and sorcery, considered by the most cultured and learned people as relics of ancient ignorance and superstition?

THEO. Let me remind you that this remark of yours cuts both ways. The "most cultured and learned" among you regard also Christianity and every other religion as a relic of ignorance and superstition. There are very good and pure Theosophists who may believe in the supernatural, divine *miracles* included, but no Occultist will do so. For an Occultist practises *scientific* Theosophy, based on accurate knowledge of Nature's secret workings; but a Theosophist, practising the powers called abnormal, *minus* the light of Occultism, will simply tend towards a dangerous form of mediumship, because, although holding to Theosophy and its highest conceivable code of ethics, he practises it in the dark, on sincere but *blind* faith.

THE DIFFERENCE BETWEEN THEOSOPHY AND SPIRITUALISM

ENQ. But do you not believe in Spiritualism?

THEO. If by "Spiritualism" you mean the explanation which Spiritualists give of some abnormal phenomena, then decidedly *we do not*. They maintain that these manifestations are all produced by the "spirits" of departed mortals, generally their relatives, who return to earth, they say, to communicate with those they have loved or to whom they are attached. We assert that the spirits of the dead cannot return to earth — save in rare and exceptional cases; nor do they communicate with men except by *entirely subjective means.* That which does appear objectively, is only the phantom of the ex-physical man.

ENQ. Do you reject the phenomena also?

THEO. Assuredly not — save cases of conscious fraud.

ENQ. How do you account for them, then?

THEO. In many ways. The causes of such manifestations are by no means so simple as the Spiritualists would like to believe. Foremost of all, the *deus ex machina* of the so-called "materializations" is usually the astral body or "double" of the medium or of some one present.

ENQ. You say "usually"; then *what* is it that produces the rest?

THEO. That depends on the nature of the manifestations. Sometimes the astral remains, the *Kama-lokic* "shells" of the vanished *personalities* that were; at other times, Elementals. The Conscious *Individuality* of the disembodied *cannot materialize,* nor can it return from its own mental Devachanic sphere to the plane of terrestrial objectivity.

ENQ. But many of the communications received from the "spirits" show not only intelligence, but a knowledge of facts not known to the medium, and sometimes even not consciously present to the mind of the investigator, or any of those who compose the audience.

THEO. This does not necessarily prove that the intelligence and knowledge you speak of belong to *spirits,* or emanate from *disembodied* souls. Somnambulists have been known to compose music and poetry and to solve mathematical problems while in their trance state, without having ever learnt music or mathematics. Others answered intelligently to questions put to them and even, in several cases, spoke languages, such as Hebrew and Latin, of which they were entirely ignorant when awake — all this in a state of profound sleep. Will you, then, maintain that this was caused by "spirits"?

ENQ. But how would you explain it?

THEO. We assert that the divine spark in man being one and identical in its essence with the Universal Spirit, our "spiritual Self" is practically omniscient, but that it cannot manifest its knowledge owing to the impediments of matter. Now the more these impediments are removed, in other words, the more the physical body is paralysed, as to its own independent activity and consciousness, as in deep sleep or deep trance, or, again, in illness, the more fully can the *inner* Self manifest on this plane. This is our explanation of those truly wonderful phenomena of a higher order, in which undeniable intelligence and knowledge are exhibited. As to the lower order of manifestations, such as physical phenomena and the platitudes and common talk of the general "spirit," to explain even the most important of the teachings we hold upon the subject would take up more space and time than can be allotted to it at present.

ENQ. I was told that the Theosophical Society was originally founded to crush Spiritualism and belief in the survival of the individuality in man?

THEO. You are misinformed. Our beliefs are all founded on that immortal individuality. But then, like so many others, you confuse *personality* with individuality. Yet it is precisely that difference which gives the keynote to the understanding of Eastern philosophy, and which lies at the root of the divergence between the Theosophical and Spiritualistic teachings.

ENQ. Please explain your idea more clearly.

THEO. What I mean is that though our teachings insist upon the identity of spirit and matter, and though we say that spirit is *potential* matter, and matter simply crystallized spirit (*e.g.,* as ice is solidified steam), yet since the original and eternal condition of *all* is not spirit but *meta*-spirit, so to speak (visible and solid matter being simply its periodical manifestation), we maintain that the term spirit can only be applied to the *true* individuality.

ENQ. But what is the distinction between this "true individuality" and the "I" or "Ego" of which we are all conscious?

THEO. Before I can answer you, we must argue upon what you mean by "I" or "Ego."* We distinguish between the simple fact of self-consciousness, the simple feeling that "I am I," and the complex thought that "I am Mr. Smith" or "Mrs. Brown." Believing as we do in a series of births for the same Ego, or reincarnation, this distinction is the fundamental pivot of the whole idea. You see "Mr. Smith" really means a long series of daily experiences strung together by the thread of memory, and forming what Mr. Smith calls "himself." But none of these "experiences" are really the "I" or the Ego, nor do they give Mr. Smith the feeling that he is himself, for he forgets the greater part of his daily experiences, and they produce the feeling of *Egoity* in him only while they last. We Theosophists, therefore, distinguish between this bundle of "experiences," which we call the *false* (because so finite and evanescent) *personality,* and that element in man to which the feeling of "I am I" is due. It is this "I am I" which we call the *true* individuality; and we say that this Ego or individuality plays, like an actor, many parts on the stage of life.† Let us call every new life on earth of the same *Ego* a *night* on the stage of a theatre. One night the actor, or Ego, appears as Macbeth, the next as Shylock, the third as Romeo, the fourth as Hamlet or King Lear, and so on, until he has run through the whole cycle of incarnations. The Ego begins his life-pilgrimage as a sprite, an Ariel, or a Puck; he plays the part of a *super,* is a soldier, a servant, one of the chorus; rises then to speaking parts, plays leading *roles,* interspersed with insignificant parts, till he finally retires from the stage as Prospero, the *magician.*

*[The word "Ego" as used here should not be confused with the use of the term in modern psychology. — Ed.]

† *Vide infra,* "On Individuality and Personality."

ENQ. I understand. You say, then, that this true *Ego* cannot return to earth after death. But surely the actor is at liberty, if he has preserved the sense of his individuality, to return if he likes to the scene of his former actions?

THEO. We say not, simply because such a return to earth would be incompatible with any state of *unalloyed* bliss after death, as I am prepared to prove.

WHY IS THEOSOPHY ACCEPTED?

ENQ. I understand to a certain extent; but I see that your teachings are far more complicated and metaphysical than either Spiritualism or current religious thought. Can you tell me, then, what has caused this system of Theosophy which you support to arouse so much interest and so much animosity at the same time?

THEO. There are several reasons for it, I believe; among other causes may be mentioned is, *first,* the great reaction from the crassly materialistic theories prevalent among scientific teachers. *Secondly,* general dissatisfaction with the theology of the various Christian Churches. *Thirdly,* an ever-growing perception of the fact that the creeds which are so obviously self — and mutually — contradictory *cannot be true,* and that claims which are unverified *cannot be real. Fourthly,* a conviction on the part of many, and *knowledge* by a few, that there must be somewhere a philosophical and religious system which shall be scientific and not merely speculative. *Finally,* a belief, perhaps, that such a system must be sought for in teachings far antedating any modern faith.

ENQ. But how did this system come to be put forward just now?

THEO. Just because the time was found to be ripe, which fact is shown by the determined effort of so many earnest students to reach *the truth,* at whatever cost and wherever it may be concealed. Seeing this, its custodians permitted that some portions at least of that truth should be proclaimed.

ENQ. Are we to regard Theosophy in any way as a revelation?

THEO. In no way whatever — not even in the sense of a new and direct disclosure from some higher, supernatural, or, at least, *superhuman beings;* but only in the sense of an "unveiling" of old, very old, truths to minds hitherto ignorant of them, ignorant even of the existence and preservation of any such archaic knowledge.

ENQ. If truth is as represented by Theosophy, why has it met with such opposition, and with no general accept-ance?

THEO. For many and various reasons again, one of which is the hatred felt by men for "innovations," as they call them. Selfishness is essentially conservative, and hates being disturbed. It prefers an easy-going, unexacting *lie* to the greatest truth, if the latter requires the sacrifice of one's smallest comfort. The power of mental inertia is great in anything that does not promise immediate benefit and reward. Moreover, there is the unfamiliar character of Theosophic teachings; the highly abstruse nature of the doctrines, some of which contradict flatly many of the human vagaries cherished by sectarians. If we add to this the personal efforts and great purity of life exacted of those to which an entirely unselfish code appeals, it will be easy to perceive the reason why Theosophy is doomed to such slow, uphill work. It is essentially the philosophy of those who suffer, and have lost all hope of being helped out of the mire of life by any other means. Moreover, the history of any system of belief or morals, newly introduced into a foreign soil, shows that its beginnings were impeded by every obsta-cle that obscurantism and selfishness could suggest.

III

THE WORKING SYSTEM OF THE T.S.

THE OBJECTS OF THE SOCIETY

ENQ. What are the objects of the Theosophical Society?

THEO. They are three, and have been so from the beginning.
(1) To form the nucleus of a Universal Brotherhood of
Humanity without distinction of race, colour, or creed.
(2) To promote the study of the world's religion and
sciences, and to vindicate the importance of old Asiatic
literature, namely, of the Brahmanical, Buddhist, and
Zoroastrian philosophies. (3) To investigate the hidden
mysteries of Nature under every aspect possible, and
the psychic and spiritual powers latent in man especially. These are, broadly stated, the three chief objects
of the Theosophical Society.*

ENQ. Can you give me some more detailed information
upon these?

THEO. We may divide each of the three objects into as many
explanatory clauses as may be found necessary.

ENQ. Then let us begin with the first. What means would
you resort to, in order to promote such a feeling of
brotherhood among races that are known to be of the
most diversified religions, customs, beliefs, and modes
of thought?

THEO. Allow me to add that which you seem unwilling to

---

*[Various changes occurred in the Society's objects after it was established in
1875. In 1896 the following wording was adopted and there has been
no further change since then: (1) To form a nucleus of the Universal
Brotherhood of Humanity, without distinction of race, creed, sex,
caste, or color. (2) To encourage the study of comparative religion,
philosophy and science. (3) To investigate unexplained laws of nature
and the powers latent in man. — Ed.]

express. Of course we know that every nation is divided, not merely against all other nations, but even against itself. Hence your wonder, and the reason why our first object appears to you a Utopia. Is it not so?

ENQ. Well, yes; but what have you to say against it?

THEO. Nothing against the fact; but much about the necessity of removing the causes which make Universal Brotherhood a Utopia at present.

ENQ. What are, in your view, these causes?

THEO. First and foremost, the natural selfishness of human nature. All the unselfishness of the altruistic teachings of Jesus has become merely a theoretical subject for pulpit oratory; while the precepts of practical selfishness, against which Christ so vainly preached, have become ingrained into the innermost life of the Western nations. "An eye for an eye and a tooth for a tooth" has come to be the first maxim of your law. Now, I state openly and fearlessly that the perversity of this doctrine and of so many others *Theosophy alone* can eradicate.

THE COMMON ORIGIN OF MAN

ENQ. How?

THEO. Simply by demonstrating on logical, philosophical, metaphysical, and even scientific grounds that: (*a*) All men have spiritually and physically the same origin, which is the fundamental teaching of Theosophy. (*b*) As mankind is essentially of one and the same essence, and that essence is one — infinite, uncreate, and eternal, whether we call it God or Nature — nothing, therefore, can affect one nation or one man without affecting all other nations and all other men.

ENQ. But this is not the teaching of Christ, but rather a pantheistic notion.

THEO. That is where your mistake lies. It is purely *Christian*.

ENQ. Where are your proofs for such a statement?

THEO. They are ready at hand. Christ is alleged to have said: "Love each other" and "Love your enemies"; for "if ye love them (only) which love you, what reward (or merit) have ye? Do not even the *publicans** the same? And if you salute your brethren only, what do ye more than others? Do not even publicans so?" These are Christ's words. But *Genesis*, ix, 25, says "Cursed be Canaan; a servant of servants shall he be upon his brethren." And, therefore, Biblical people prefer the law of Moses to Christ's law of love. They base upon the Old Testament, which panders to all their passions, their laws of conquest, annexation, and tyranny over races which they call *inferior*. What crimes have been committed on the strength of this infernal (if taken in its dead letter) passage in Genesis, history alone gives us an idea, however inadequate.

ENQ. I have heard you say that the identity of our physical origin is proved by science, that of our spiritual origin by the Wisdom-Religion. Yet we do not find Darwinists exhibiting great fraternal affection.

THEO. This is what shows the deficiency of the materialistic systems, and proves that we Theosophists are in the right. The identity of our physical origin makes no appeal to our higher and deeper feelings. Matter, deprived of its soul and spirit, or its divine essence, cannot speak to the human heart. But the identity of the soul and spirit, of real, immortal man, as Theosophy teaches us, once proven and deep-rooted in our hearts, would lead us far on the road of real charity and brotherly goodwill.

---

* Publicans — regarded as so many thieves and pickpockets in these days. Among the Jews the name and profession of a publican was the most odious thing in the world. They were not allowed to enter the Temple, and *Matthew* (xviii, 17) speaks of a heathen and a publican as identical. Yet they were only Roman tax-gatherers.

ENQ. But how does Theosophy explain the common origin of man?

THEO. By teaching that the *root* of all nature, objective and subjective, and everything else in the universe, visible and invisible, *is, was,* and *ever will be* one absolute essence, from which all starts, and into which everything returns.

ENQ. What do the statutes of your Society advise its members to do besides this? On the physical plane, I mean?

THEO. In order to awaken brotherly feeling among nations we have to assist in the international exchange of useful arts and products, by advice, information, and cooperation with all worthy individuals and associations. What is also needed is to impress men with the idea that, if the root of mankind is *one,* then there must also be one truth which finds expression in all the various religions.

ENQ. This refers to the common origin of religions, and you may be right there. But how does it apply to practical brotherhood on the physical plane?

THEO. First, because that which is true on the metaphysical plane must be also true on the physical. Secondly, because there is no more fertile source of hatred and strife than religious differences. When one party or another thinks himself the sole possessor of absolute truth, it becomes only natural that he should think his neighbour absolutely in the clutches of Error or the Devil. But once get a man to see that none of them has the *whole* truth, but that they are mutually complementary, that the complete truth can be found only in the combined views of all, after that which is false in each of them has been sifted out — then true brotherhood in religion will be established. The same applies in the physical world.

ENQ. Please explain further.

THEO. Take an instance. A plant consists of a root, a stem,

and many shoots and leaves. As humanity, as a whole, is the stem which grows from the spiritual root, so is the stem the unity of the plant. Hurt the stem and it is obvious that every shoot and leaf will suffer. So it is with mankind.

ENQ. Yes, but if you injure a leaf or a shoot, you do not injure the whole plant.

THEO. And therefore you think that by injuring *one* man you do not injure humanity? But how do *you* know? Are you aware that even materialistic science teaches that any injury, however slight, to a plant will affect the whole course of its future growth and development? If you overlook the fact that a cut in the finger may often make the whole body suffer, and react on the whole nervous system, I must all the more remind you that there may well be other spiritual laws, operating on plants and animals as well as on mankind, although, as you do not recognize their action on plants and animals, you may deny their existence.

ENQ. What laws do you mean?

THEO. We call them Karmic laws; but you will not understand the full meaning of the term unless you study Occultism. However, my argument did not rest on the assumption of these laws, but really on the analogy of the plant. Expand the idea, carry it out to a universal application, and you will soon find that in true philosophy every physical action has its moral and everlasting effect. Hurt a man by doing him bodily harm; you may think that his pain and suffering cannot spread by any means to his neighbours, least of all to men of other nations. We affirm *that it will, in good time.* Therefore, we say, that unless every man is brought to understand and accept *as an axiomatic truth* that by wronging one man we wrong not only ourselves but the whole of humanity in the long run, no brotherly feelings such as preached by all the great Reformers, pre-eminently by Buddha and Jesus, are possible on earth.

OUR OTHER OBJECTS

ENQ. Will you now explain the methods by which you propose to carry out the second object?

THEO. To collect for the library at our headquarters of Adyar, Madras (and by the Fellows of their Branches for their local libraries), all the good works upon the world's religions that we can. To put into written form correct information upon the various ancient philosophies, traditions, and legends, and disseminate the same in such practicable ways as the translation and publication of original works of value, and extracts from and commentaries upon the same, or the oral instructions of persons learned in their respective departments.

ENQ. And what about the third object, to develop in man his latent spiritual or psychic powers?

THEO. This has to be achieved also by means of publications, in those places where no lectures and personal teachings are possible. Our duty is to keep alive in man his spiritual intuitions. To oppose and counteract — after due investigation and proof of its irrational nature — bigotry in every form, religious, scientific, or social, and *cant* above all, whether as religious sectarianism or as belief in miracles or anything supernatural. What we have to do is to seek to obtain *knowledge* of all the laws of nature, and to diffuse it. To encourage the study of those laws least understood by modern people, the so-called Occult Sciences, *based on the true knowledge of nature*. Popular folk-lore and traditions, however fanciful at times, when sifted may lead to the discovery of long-lost, but important, secrets of nature. The Society, therefore, aims at pursuing this line of enquiry, in the hope of widening the field of scientific and philosophical observation.

IV

THE RELATIONS OF THE THEOSOPHICAL SOCIETY TO THEOSOPHY

ON SELF-IMPROVEMENT

ENQ. Is moral elevation, then, the principal thing insisted upon in your Society?

THEO. Undoubtedly! He who would be a true Theosophist must bring himself to live as one.

ENQ. If so, then, as I remarked before, the behaviour of some members strangely belies this fundamental rule.

THEO. Indeed it does. But this cannot be helped among us, any more than among those who call themselves Christians and act like fiends. This is no fault of our statutes and rules, but that of human nature. A true Theosophist ought "to deal justly and walk humbly."

ENQ. What do you mean by this?

THEO. Simply this: the one self has to forget itself for the many selves.

ENQ. This is pure altruism, I confess.

THEO. It is. And if only one Fellow of the T. S. out of ten would practise it ours would be a body of elect indeed. But there are those among the outsiders who will always refuse to see the essential difference between Theosophy and the Theosophical Society, the idea and its imperfect embodiment.

ENQ. Yet it is rather difficult to draw the line of demarcation between the abstract and the concrete in this case, as we have only the latter to form our judgement by.

THEO. Justice, like charity, ought to begin at home. Will

you revile and scoff at the Sermon on the Mount because your social, political and even religious laws have,
so far, not only failed to carry out its precepts in their
spirit, but even in their dead letter? "Resist not evil,
love your enemies, bless them that curse you, do good
to them that hate you," for "whosoever shall break one
of the least of these Commandments and shall teach men
so, he shall be called the least in the Kingdom of
Heaven," and "whosoever shall say 'Thou fool' shall
be in danger of hell fire." And why should you judge,
if you would not be judged in your turn? Insist that
between Theosophy and the Theosophical Society there
is no difference, and forthwith you lay the system of
Christianity and its very essence open to the same
charges. It cannot be too often repeated that between
the abstract ideal and its vehicle there is a most important difference.

THE ABSTRACT AND THE CONCRETE

ENQ. Please elucidate this difference a little more.

THEO. The Society is a great body of men and women, composed of the most heterogeneous elements. Theosophy,
in its abstract meaning, is Divine Wisdom, or the aggregate of the knowledge and wisdom that underlie the
Universe — the homogeneity of eternal GOOD; and in its
concrete sense it is the sum total of the same as allotted
to man by nature, on this earth, and no more. Some
members earnestly endeavour to realize and, so to speak,
to objectivize Theosophy in their lives; while others
desire only to know of, not to practise it; and others still
may have joined the Society merely out of curiosity, or
a passing interest, or perhaps, again, because some of
their friends belong to it. How, then, can the system
be judged by the standard of those who would assume
the name without any right to it? The Society can be
regarded as the embodiment of Theosophy only in its
abstract motives; it can never presume to call itself its

concrete vehicle so long as human imperfections and weaknesses are all represented in its body. If Eastern comparisons may be permitted, Theosophy is the shoreless ocean of universal truth, love, and wisdom, reflecting its radiance on the earth, while the Theosophical Society is only a visible bubble on that reflection. Theosophy is divine nature, visible and invisible, and its Society human nature trying to ascend to its divine parent. Theosophy, finally, is the fixed eternal sun, and its Society the evanescent comet trying to settle in an orbit to become a planet, ever revolving within the attraction of the sun of truth. It was formed to assist in showing to men that such a thing as Theosophy exists, and to help them to ascend towards it by studying and assimilating its eternal verities.

ENQ. I thought you said you had no tenets or doctrines of your own?

THEO. No more we have. The Society has no wisdom of its own to support or teach. It is simply the storehouse of all the truths uttered by the great seers, initiates, and prophets of historic and even prehistoric ages; at least, as many as it can get. Therefore, it is merely the channel through which more or less of truth, found in the accumulated utterances of humanity's great teachers, is poured out into the world.

ENQ. But is such truth unreachable outside of the society?

THEO. The undeniable existence of great initiates — true "Sons of God" — shows that such wisdom was often reached by isolated individuals, never, however, without the guidance of a master at first. But most of the followers of such, when they became masters in their turn, have dwarfed the catholicism of these teachings into the narrow groove of their own sectarian dogmas. The commandments of *a* chosen master alone were then adopted and followed, to the exclusion of all others — if followed at all, note well, as in the case of the Sermon on the Mount. Each religion is thus a bit of the divine truth, made to focus a vast panorama of human fancy which claimed to represent and replace that truth.

ENQ. But Theosophy, you say, is not a religion?

THEO. Most assuredly it is not, since it is the essence of all religion and of absolute truth, a drop of which only underlies every creed. To resort once more to metaphor. Theosophy, on earth, is like the white ray of the spectrum, and every religion only one of the seven prismatic colours. Ignoring all the others, and cursing them as false, every special coloured ray claims not only priority, but to be *that white ray* itself, and anathematizes even its own tints from light to dark, as heresies. Yet, as the sun of truth rises higher and higher on the horizon of man's perception, and each coloured ray gradually fades out until it is finally reabsorbed in its turn, humanity will at last be cursed no longer with artificial polarizations, but will find itself bathing in the pure colourless sunlight of eternal truth. And this will be *Theosophia*.

ENQ. Your claim is, then, that all the great religions are derived from Theosophy, and that it is by assimilating it that the world will be finally saved from the curse of its great illusions and errors?

THEO. Precisely so. And we add that our Theosophical Society is the humble seed which, if watered and left to live, will finally produce the Tree of Knowledge of Good and Evil which is grafted on the Tree of Life Eternal. For it is only by studying the various great religions and philosophies of humanity, by comparing them dispassionately and with an unbiased mind, that men can hope to arrive at the truth. It is especially by finding out and noting their various points of agreement that we may achieve this result. For no sooner do we arrive — either by study, or by being taught by someone who knows — at their inner meaning, that we find, almost in every case, that it expresses some great truth in Nature.

ENQ. We have heard of a Golden Age that was, and what you describe would be a Golden Age to be realized at some future day. When shall it be?

THEO. Not before humanity, as a whole, feels the need of it. A maxim in the Persian *Javidan Kherad* says: "Truth is of two kinds — one manifest and self-evident; the other demanding incessantly new demonstrations and proofs." It is only when this latter kind of truth becomes as universally obvious as it is now dim, and therefore liable to be distorted by sophistry and casuistry; it is only when the two kinds will have become once more one, that all people will be brought to see alike.

ENQ. But surely those few who have felt the need of such truths must have made up their minds to believe in something definite? You tell me that, the Society having no doctrines of its own, every member may believe as he chooses and accept what he pleases. This looks as if the Theosophical Society was bent upon reviving the confusion of languages and beliefs of the Tower of Babel of old. Have you no beliefs in common?

THEO. What is meant by the Society having no tenets or doctrines of its own is, that no special doctrines or beliefs are *obligatory* on its members.

V

THE FUNDAMENTAL TEACHINGS OF THEOSOPHY

ON GOD AND PRAYER

ENQ. Do you believe in God?

THEO. That depends what you mean by the term.

ENQ. I mean the God of the Christians, the Father of Jesus, and the Creator: the Biblical God of Moses, in short.

THEO. In such a God we do not believe. We reject the idea of a personal, or an extra-cosmic and anthropomorphic God, who is but the gigantic shadow of *man,* and not of man at his best, either. The God of theology, we say is a bundle of contradictions and a logical impossibility. Therefore we will have nothing to do with him.

ENQ. State your reasons, if you please.

THEO. They are many, and cannot all receive attention. But here are a few. This God is called by his devotees infinite and absolute, is he not?

ENQ. I believe he is.

THEO. Then, if infinite — *i.e.,* limitless — and especially if ab-

solute, how can he have a form, and be a creator of anything? Form implies limitation, and a beginning as well
as an end; and, in order to create, a Being must think
and plan. How can the ABSOLUTE be supposed to
think — *i.e.* to have any relation whatever to that which
is limited, finite, and conditioned? This is a philosophical and a logical absurdity. Even the Hebrew Kabala re-
jects such an idea, and therefore makes of the one and
the Absolute Deific Principle an infinite Unity called
Ain-Soph.* In order to create, the Creator has to become
active; and as this is impossible for ABSOLUTENESS,
the infinite principle had to be shown becoming the
cause of evolution (not creation) in an indirect way —
i.e., through the emanation from itself (another absurdity, due this time to the translators of the Kabala) † of
the Sephiroth.

ENQ. Then you are Atheists?

THEO. Not that we know of, and not unless the epithet of
Atheist is to be applied to those who disbelieve in an
anthropomorphic God. We believe in a Universal Divine Principle, the root of ALL, from which all proceeds, and within which all shall be absorbed at the end
of the great cycle of Being.

ENQ. This is the old, old claim of Pantheism. If you are
Pantheists, you cannot be Deists; and if you are not
Deists, then you have to answer to the name of Atheist.

THEO. Not necessarily so. The term Pantheism is again one
of the many abused terms, whose real and primitive
meaning has been distorted by blind prejudice and a
one-sided view of it. If you accept the Christian etymo-

---

* Ain-Soph, אין סוף =τὸ πᾶυ= ὁ ἄπειρος, the endless, or boundless, in and
    with Nature, the non-existent which IS, but is not *a* Being.

†How can the non-active eternal principle emanate or emit? The Parabrahm
    of the Vedantins does nothing of the kind; nor does the Ain-Soph of
    the Chaldean Kabala. It is an eternal and periodical law which causes
    an active and creative force (the logos) to emanate from the ever-
    concealed and incomprehensible one principle at the beginning of
    every mahamanvantara, or new cycle of life.

logy of this compound word, and form it of πᾶν, "all,"
and θεός, "god," and then imagine and teach that this
means that every stone and every tree in Nature is a God
or the ONE God, then, of course, you will be right, and
make of Pantheists fetish-worshippers, in addition to
their legitimate name. But you will hardly be as successful if you etymologize the word Pantheism esoterically,
and as we do.

ENQ. What is, then, your definition of it?

THEO. Let me ask you a question in my turn. What do you
understand by Pan, or Nature?

ENQ. Nature is, I suppose, the sum total of things existing
around us; the aggregate of causes and effects in the
world of matter, the creation or universe.

THEO. Hence the personified sum and order of known causes
and effects; the total of all finite agencies and forces, as
utterly disconnected from an intelligent Creator or
Creators, and perhaps "conceived of as a single and
separate force" — as in your cyclopaedias?

ENQ. Yes, I believe so.

THEO. Well, we neither take into consideration this objective and material nature, which we call an evanescent
illusion, nor do we mean by πᾶν Nature, in the sense
of its accepted derivation from the Latin *Natura* (becoming, from *nasci*, to be born). When we speak of the
Deity and make it identical, hence coeval, with Nature,
the eternal and uncreate nature is meant, and not your
aggregate of flitting shadows and finite unrealities. Our
DEITY is everywhere, in every atom of the visible as
of the invisible Cosmos, in, over, and around every invisible atom and divisible molecule; for IT is the mysterious power of evolution and involution, the omnipresent, omnipotent, and even omniscient creative po-
tentiality.

ENQ. Omniscience is the prerogative of something that

thinks, and you deny to your Absoluteness the power of thought.

THEO. We deny it to the ABSOLUTE, since thought is something limited and conditioned. But you evidently forget that in philosophy absolute unconsciousness is also consciousness, as otherwise it would not be *absolute*.

ENQ. Then your Absolute thinks?

THEO. No, IT does not; for the simple reason that it is *Absolute Thought* itself. Nor does it exist, for the same reason, as it is absolute existence, and *Be-ness,* not a Being. Read the superb Kabalistic poem by Solomon Ben Yehudah Gebirol, in the *Kether-Malkûth,* and you will understand: "Thou art one, the root of all numbers, but not as an element of numeration; for unity admits not of multiplication, change, or form. Thou art one, and in the secret of thy unity the wisest of men are lost, because they know it not. Thou art one, and thy unity is never diminished, never extended, and cannot be changed. Thou art one, and no thought of mine can fix for thee a limit, or define thee. Thou ART, but not as one existent, for the understanding and vision of mortals cannot attain to thy existence, nor determine for thee the where, the how and the why," etc., etc. In short, our Deity is the eternal, incessantly *evolving,* not *creating,* builder of the universe; that *universe itself unfolding* out of its own essence, not being *made.* It is a sphere, without circumference, in its symbolism, which has but one ever acting attribute embracing all other existing or thinkable attributes — ITSELF. It is the one law, giving the impulse to manifested, eternal, and immutable laws, within that never-manifesting, *because* absolute LAW, which in its manifesting periods is *The ever-Becoming.*

IS IT NECESSARY TO PRAY?

ENQ. Do you believe in prayer, and do you ever pray?

THEO. We do not. We *act,* instead of *talking.*

ENQ. You do not offer prayers even to the Absolute Principle?

THEO. Why should we? The Unknowable is capable of relations only in its parts to each other, but is non-existent as regards any finite relations. The visible universe depends for its existence and phenomena on its mutually acting forms and their laws, not on prayer or prayers.

ENQ. Do you not believe at all in the efficacy of prayer?

THEO. Not in prayer taught in so many words and repeated externally, if by prayer you mean the outward petition to an unknown God as the addressee.

ENQ. Is there any other kind of prayer?

THEO. Most decidedly; we call it WILL-PRAYER, and it is rather an internal command than a petition.

ENQ. To whom, then, do you *pray* when you do so?

THEO. To "our Father in heaven" — in its esoteric meaning.

ENQ. Is that different from the one given to it in theology?

THEO. Entirely so. An Occultist or a Theosophist addresses his prayer to *his Father which is in secret* (read, and try to understand, *Matthew* vi, 6), not to an extra-cosmic and therefore finite God; and that "Father" is in man himself.

ENQ. Then you make of man a God?

THEO. Please say "God" and not *a* God. In our sense, the inner man is the only God we can have cognizance of. And how can this be otherwise? Grant us our postulate that God is a universally diffused, infinite principle, and how can man alone escape from being soaked through *by*, and *in*, the Deity? We call our "Father in heaven" that deific essence of which we are cognizant within us, in our heart and spiritual consciousness, and which has nothing to do with the anthropomorphic conception we may form of it in our physical brain or its fancy: "Know ye not that ye are the temple of God, and that the spirit of [the absolute] God dwelleth in you?"* Yet, let no man anthropomorphize that essence in us. Let no Theosophist, if he would hold to divine, not human truth, say that this "God in secret" listens to, or is distinct from, either finite man or the infinite essence — for all are one. Nor, as just remarked, that a prayer is a petition. It is a mystery rather; an occult process by which finite and conditioned thoughts and desires, unable to be assimilated by the absolute spirit which is unconditioned, are translated into spiritual wills and the will; such process being called "spiritual transmutation." The intensity of our ardent aspirations changes prayer into the "philosopher's stone," or that which transmutes lead into pure gold. The only homogeneous essence, our "will-prayer" becomes the active or creative force, producing effects according to our desire.

ENQ. Do you mean to say that prayer is an occult process bringing about physical results?

THEO. I do. *Will-Power* becomes a living power. But woe unto those Occultists and Theosophists who, instead of crushing out the desires of the lower personal *ego* or physical man and saying, addressing their *Higher* Spiritual EGO immersed in Atma-Buddhic light, "Thy will be done, not mine," etc., send up waves of will-power for selfish or unholy purposes! For this is black magic, abomination, and spiritual sorcery.

---

* *I Cor.*, iii, 16] One often finds in Theosophical writings conflicting statements about the Christos principle in man. Some call it the sixth principle (*Buddhi*), others the seventh (*Atman*). If Christian Theosophists wish to make use of such expressions, let them be made philosophically correct by following the analogy of the old Wisdom-religion symbols. We say that Christos is not only one of the three higher principles, but all the three regarded as a Trinity. This Trinity represents the Holy Ghost, the Father, and the Son, as it answers to abstract spirit, differentiated spirit, and embodied spirit. Krishna and Christ are philosophically the same principle under its triple aspect of manifestation. In the *Bhagavad Gita* we find Krishna calling himself indifferently Atman, the abstract Spirit, Kshetrajna, the Higher or reincarnating Ego, and the Universal SELF, all names which, when transferred from the Universe to man, answer to *Atma, Buddhi* and *Manas*. The *Anugita* is full of the same doctrine.

ENQ. How do you explain the universal fact that all nations and peoples have prayed to, and worshipped a God or Gods? Some have adored and propitiated *devils* and harmful spirits, but this only proves the universality of the belief in the efficacy of prayer.

THEO. It is explained by that other fact that prayer has several other meanings besides that given it by the Christians. It means not only a pleading or *petition*, but meant, in days of old, far more an invocation and incantation. The *mantra*, or the rhythmically chanted prayer of the Hindus, has precisely such a meaning, as the Brahmins hold themselves higher than the common *devas* or "Gods." A prayer may be an appeal or an incantation for malediction, and a curse (as in the case of two armies praying simultaneously for mutual destruction) as much as for blessing. And as the great majority of people are intensely selfish, and pray only for themselves, asking to be *given* their "daily bread" instead of working for it, and begging God not to lead them "into temptation" but to deliver them from evil, the result is, that prayer, as now understood, is doubly pernicious: (*a*) It kills in man self-reliance; (*b*) It develops in him a still more ferocious selfishness and egotism than he is already endowed with by nature. I repeat, that we believe in "communion" and simultaneous action in unison with our "Father in secret"; and in rare moments of ecstatic bliss, in the mingling of our higher soul with the universal essence, attracted as it is towards its origin and centre, a state, called during life *Samadhi*, and after death *Nirvana*. We refuse to pray to *created* finite beings — *i.e.*, gods, saints, angels, etc., because we regard it as idolatry. We cannot pray to the ABSOLUTE for reasons explained before; therefore, we try to replace fruitless and useless prayer by meritorious and good-producing actions.

PRAYER KILLS SELF-RELIANCE

ENQ. But did not Christ himself pray and recommend prayer?

THEO. It is so recorded, but those "prayers" are precisely of that kind of communion just mentioned with one's "Father in secret." Otherwise, and if we identify Jesus with the universal deity, there would be something too absurdly illogical in the inevitable conclusion that he, the "very God himself" *prayed to himself,* and separated the will of that God from his own!

ENQ. One argument more: an argument, moreover, much used by some Christians. They say, "I feel that I am not able to conquer any passions and weaknesses in my own strength. But when I pray to Jesus Christ I feel that he gives me strength and that in his power I am able to conquer."

THEO. No wonder. If "Christ Jesus" is God, and one independent and separate from him who prays, of course everything is, and *must* be possible to "almighty God." But, then, where's the merit, or justice either, of such a conquest? Why should the pseudo-conqueror be rewarded for something done which has cost him only prayers? Would you, even a simple mortal man, pay your labourer a full day's wage if you did most of his work for him, he sitting under an apple tree, and praying to you to do so, all the while? This idea of passing one's whole life in moral idleness, and having one's hardest work and duty done by another — whether God or man — is most revolting to us, as it is most degrading to human dignity.

ENQ. Where does a Theosophist look to for power to subdue his passions and selfishness?

THEO. To his Higher Self, the divine spirit, or the God in him, and to his *Karma.* How long shall we have to repeat over and over again that the tree is known by its fruit, the nature of the cause by its effects?

ON THE SOURCE OF THE HUMAN SOUL

ENQ. How, then, do you account for man being endowed with a Spirit and Soul? Whence these?

THEO. From the Universal Soul. Certainly not bestowed by a *personal* God. Whence the moist element in the jellyfish? From the Ocean which surrounds it, in which it lives and breathes and has its being, and whither it returns when dissolved.

ENQ. So you reject the teaching that Soul is given, or breathed into man, by God?

THEO. We are obliged to. The "Soul" spoken of in ch. ii, 7, of *Genesis* is, as therein stated, the "living Soul" or *Nephesh* (the *vital,* animal soul) with which God (we say "nature" and *immutable law*) endows man like every animal; is not at all the thinking soul or mind; least of all is it the *immortal Spirit.*

ENQ. Well, let us put it otherwise: is it God who endows man with a human *rational* Soul and immortal Spirit?

THEO. Again, in the way you put the question, we must object to it. Since we believe in no *personal* God, how can we believe that he endows man with anything? But granting, for the sake of argument, a God who takes upon himself the risk of creating a new Soul for every new-born baby, all that can be said is that such a God can hardly be regarded as himself endowed with any wisdom or prevision. Certain other difficulties and the impossibility of reconciling this with the claims made for the mercy, justice, equity and omniscience of that God are so many deadly reefs on which this theological dogma is daily and hourly broken.

ENQ. What do you mean? What difficulties?

THEO. I am thinking of an unanswerable argument offered once by a Sinhalese Buddhist priest, a famous preacher, to a Christian missionary — one in no way ignorant or unprepared for the public discussion during which it was advanced. It was near Colombo, and the missionary had challenged the priest Megituwatte to give his reasons why the Christian God should not be accepted by the "heathen." Well, the missionary came out of that for ever memorable discussion second best, as usual.

ENQ. I should be glad to learn in what way.

THEO. Simply this: the Buddhist priest premised by asking the padre whether his God had given commandments to Moses only for men to keep, but to be broken by God himself. The missionary denied the supposition indignantly. Well, said his opponent, "you tell us that God makes no exceptions to this rule, and that no Soul can be born without his will. Now God forbids adultery, among other things, and yet you say in the same breath that it is he who creates every baby born, and he who endows it with a Soul. Are we then to understand that the millions of children born in crime and adultery are your God's work? That your God forbids and punishes the breaking of his laws; and that, nevertheless, *he creates daily and hourly souls for just such children?* According to the simplest logic, your God is an accomplice in the crime; since, but for his help and interference, no such children of lust could be born. Where is the justice of punishing not only the guilty parents but even the innocent babe for that which is done by that very God whom yet you exonerate from any guilt himself?" The missionary looked at his watch and suddenly found it was getting too late for further discussion.

ENQ. You forget that all such inexplicable cases are mysteries, and that we are forbidden by our religion to pry into the mysteries of God.

THEO. No, we do not forget, but simply reject such impossibilities. Nor do we want you to believe as we do. We only answer the questions you ask.

THE BUDDHIST TEACHINGS ON THE ABOVE

ENQ. What does Buddhism teach with regard to the Soul?

THEO. It depends whether you mean exoteric, popular Buddhism, or its esoteric teachings. The former explains itself in the *Buddhist Catechism* in this wise: "Soul it considers a word used by the ignorant to express a false idea. If everything is subject to change, then man is included, and every material part of him must change. That which is subject to change is not permanent, so there can be no immortal survival of a changeful thing." This seems plain and definite. But when we come to the question that the new personality in each succeeding rebirth is the aggregate of *Skandhas,* or the attributes, of the *old* personality, and ask whether this new aggregation of *Skandhas* is a *new* being likewise, in which nothing has remained of the last, we read that: "In one sense it is a new being, in another it is not. During this life the *Skandhas* are continually changing, while the man A. B. of forty is identical as regards personality with the youth A. B. of eighteen, yet by the continual waste and reparation of his body and change of mind and character he is a different being. Nevertheless, the man in his old age justly reaps the reward or suffering consequent upon his thoughts and actions at every previous stage of his life. So the new being of the rebirth, being the *same individuality* as before (but not the same personality), with but a changed form or new aggregation of *Skandhas,* justly reaps the consequences of his actions and thoughts in the previous existence." This is abstruse metaphysics, and plainly does not express *disbelief* in Soul by any means.

ENQ. Is not something like this spoken of in *Esoteric Buddhism?*

THEO. It is, for this teaching belongs both to Esoteric *Buddhism* or Secret Wisdom, and to the exoteric Buddhism, or the religious philosophy of Gautama Buddha.

ENQ. But we are distinctly told that most of the Buddhists do not believe in the Soul's immortality?

THEO. No more do we, if you mean by Soul the *personal Ego*, or life-Soul — *Nephesh*. But every learned Buddhist believes in the individual or *divine Ego*. Those who do not, err in their judgement. They are as mistaken on this point as those Christians who mistake the theological interpolations of the later editors of the Gospels about damnation and hell-fire for *verbatim* utterances of Jesus. Neither Buddha nor "Christ" ever wrote anything themselves, but both spoke in allegories and used "dark sayings," as all true Initiates did, and will do for a long time yet to come. Both Scriptures treat of all such metaphysical questions very cautiously, and both Buddhist and Christian records sin by that excess of exotericism; the dead letter meaning far overshooting the mark in both cases.

ENQ. Do you mean to suggest that neither the teachings of Buddha nor those of Christ have been heretofore rightly understood?

THEO. What I mean is just as you say. Both Gospels, the Buddhist and the Christian, were preached with the same object in view. Both reformers were ardent philanthropists and practical *altruists — preaching most unmistakably Socialism* of the noblest and highest type, self-sacrifice to the bitter end. "Let the sins of the whole world fall upon me that I may relieve man's misery and suffering!" cries Buddha; . . . "I would not let one cry whom I could save!" exclaims the Prince-beggar, clad in the refuse rags of the burial-grounds. "Come unto me, all ye that labour and are heavy laden, and I will give you rest,"* is the appeal to the poor and the disinherited made by the "Man of Sorrows," who had not where to lay his head. The teachings of both are boundless love for humanity, charity, forgiveness of injury, forgetfulness of self, and pity for the

---

* [*Matt.*, xi., 28.]

deluded masses; both show the same contempt for riches, and make no difference between *meum* and *tuum*. Their desire was, without revealing to *all* the sacred mysteries of initiation, to give the ignorant and the misled, whose burden in life was too heavy for them, hope enough and an inkling into the truth sufficient to support them in their heaviest hours. But the object of both Reformers was frustrated, owing to excess of zeal of their later followers. The words of the Masters having been misunderstood and misinterpreted, behold the consequences!

ENQ. But why do Buddhism and Christianity represent the two opposite poles of such belief?

THEO. Because the conditions under which they were preached were not the same. In India the Brahmins, jealous of their superior knowledge, and excluding from it every caste save their own, had driven millions of men into idolatry and almost fetishism. Buddha had to give the death-blow to an exuberance of unhealthy fancy and fanatical superstition resulting from ignorance, such as has rarely been known before or after. Better a philosophical atheism than such ignorant worship for those —

> Who cry upon their gods and are not heard.
> Or are not heeded —

and who live and die in mental despair. He had to arrest first of all this muddy torrent of superstition, to uproot *errors* before he gave out the truth. And as he could not give out *all,* for the same good reason as Jesus, who reminds *his* disciples that the Mysteries of Heaven are not for the unintelligent masses, but for the elect alone, and therefore "spake he to them in parables" (*Matt.,* xiii, 3, 11) — so his caution led Buddha *to conceal too much.* He even refused to say to the monk Vacchagotta whether there was or was not an Ego in man. When pressed to answer, "the Exalted one maintained silence."*

ENQ. This refers to Gautama, but in what way does it touch the Gospels?

THEO. Read history and think over it. At the time the events narrated in the Gospels are alleged to have happened, there was a similar intellectual fermentation taking place in the whole civilized world, only with opposite results in the East and the West. The old gods were dying out. While the civilized classes drifted in the train of the unbelieving Sadducees into materialistic negations and mere dead-letter Mosaic form in Palestine, and into moral dissolution in Rome, the lowest and poorest classes ran after sorcery and strange gods, or became hypocrites and Pharisees. Once more the time for a spiritual reform had arrived. The cruel, anthropomorphic and jealous God of the Jews, with his sanguinary laws of eye for eye and tooth for tooth, of the shedding of blood and animal sacrifice, had to be relegated to a secondary place and replaced by the merciful "Father in Secret." The latter had to be shown, not as an extra-Cosmic God, but as a divine Saviour of the

---

* Buddha gives to Ananda, his *initiated* disciple, who enquires for the reason of this silence, a plain and unequivocal answer in the dialogue translated by Oldenburg from the *Samyutta-Nikaya:* "If I, Ananda, when the wandering monk Vacchagotta asked me: "Is there the Ego?' had answered 'The Ego is,' then that, Ananda, would have confirmed the doctrine of the Samanas and Brahmanas, who believed in permanence. If I, Ananda, when the wandering monk Vacchagotta asked me, 'Is there not the Ego?' had answered, 'The Ego is not,' then that, Ananda, would have confirmed the doctrine of those who believed in annihilation. If I, Ananda, when the wandering monk Vacchagotta asked me, 'Is there the Ego?' had answered, 'The Ego is,' would that have served my end, Ananda, by producing in him the knowledge: all existences (dhamma) are non-ego? But if I, Ananda, had answered, 'The Ego is not,' then that, Ananda, would only have caused the wandering monk Vacchagotta to be thrown from one bewilderment to another: 'My Ego, did it not exist before? But now it exists no longer!'" This shows, better than anything, that Gautama Buddha withheld such difficult metaphysical doctrines from the masses in order not to perplex them more. What he meant was the difference between the personal temporary Ego and the Higher Self, which sheds its light on the imperishable Ego, the spiritual "I" of man.

man of flesh, enshrined in his own heart and soul, in the poor as in the rich. No more here than in India could the secrets of initiation be divulged, lest by giving that which is holy to the dogs, and casting pearls before swine, both the *Revealer* and the things revealed should be trodden under foot. Thus, the reticence of both Buddha and Jesus — whether the latter lived out the historic period allotted to him or not, and who equally abstained from revealing plainly the Mysteries of Life and Death — led in the one case to the blank negations of Southern Buddhism, and in the other, to the three clashing forms of the Christian Church and the 300 sects in Protestant England alone.

VI

THEOSOPHICAL TEACHINGS AS TO NATURE AND MAN

THE UNITY OF ALL IN ALL

ENQ. Having told me what God, the Soul and Man are *not*, in your views, can you inform me what they *are*, according to your teachings?

THEO. In their origin and in eternity the three, like the universe and all therein, are one with the absolute Unity, the unknowable deific essence I spoke about some time back. We believe in no *creation*, but in the periodical and consecutive appearances of the universe from the subjective on to the objective plane of being, at regular intervals of time, covering periods of immense duration.

ENQ. Can you elaborate the subject?

THEO. Take as a first comparison and a help towards a more correct conception, the solar year, and as a second, the two halves of that year, producing each a day and a night of six months' duration at the North Pole. Now imagine, if you can, instead of a Solar year of 365 days, ETERNITY. Let the sun represent the universe, and the polar days and nights of 6 months each — *days and nights lasting each 182 trillions and quadrillions of years,* instead of 182 days each. As the sun rises every morning on our *objective* horizon out of its (to us) *subjective* and antipodal space, so does the Universe emerge periodically on the plane of objectivity, issuing from that of subjectivity — the antipodes of the former. This is the "Cycle of Life." And as the sun disappears from our horizon, so does the Universe disappear at regular periods, when the "Universal night" sets in.

The Hindus call such alternations the "Days and Nights of Brahma," or the time of *Manvantara* and that of *Pralaya* (dissolution). The Westerns may call them Universal Days and Nights if they prefer. During the latter (the nights) *All is in All;* every atom is resolved into one Homogeneity.

EVOLUTION AND ILLUSION

ENQ. But who is it that creates each time the Universe?

THEO. No one creates it. Science would call the process evolution; the pre-Christian philosophers and the Orientalists called it emanation: we, Occultists and Theosophists, see in it the only universal and eternal *reality* casting a periodical reflection of *itself* on the infinite Spatial depths. This reflection, which you regard as the objective *material* universe, we consider as a temporary *illusion* and nothing else. That alone which is eternal is *real*.

ENQ. At that rate, you and I are also illusions.

THEO. As flitting personalities, today one person, tomorrow another — we are. Would you call the sudden flashes of the *aurora borealis,* the Northern lights, a "reality," though it is as real as can be while you look at it? Certainly not; it is the cause that produces it, if permanent and eternal, which is the only reality, while the other is but a passing illusion.

ENQ. All this does not explain to me how this illusion called the universe originates; how the conscious *to be,* proceeds to manifest itself from the unconsciousness that *is*.

THEO. It is *unconsciousness* only to our finite consciousness. Whether by radiation or emanation — we need not quarrel over terms — the universe passes out of its homogeneous subjectivity on to the first plane of manifestation, of which planes there are seven. With each plane it becomes more dense and material until it reaches this, our plane, on which the only world approximately

known and understood in its physical composition by
science, is the planetary or Solar system — one *sui generis,* we are told.

ENQ. What do you mean by *sui generis?*

THEO. I mean that, though the fundamental law and the
universal working of laws of Nature are uniform, still
our Solar system (like every other such system in the
millions of others in Cosmos) and even our Earth, has
its own programme of manifestations differing from the
respective programmes of all others. We speak of the
inhabitants of other planets and imagine that if they
are *men, i.e.,* thinking entities, they must be as we are.
The fancy of poets and painters and sculptors never
fails to represent even the angels as a beautiful copy of
man — *plus* wings. We say that all this is an error and a
delusion; because, if on this little earth alone one finds
such a diversity in its flora, fauna and mankind —
from the seaweed to the cedar of Lebanon, from the
jellyfish to the elephant, from the Bushman to the
Apollo Belvedere — alter the conditions cosmic and
planetary, and there must be as a result quite a different flora, fauna and mankind. The same laws will fash-
ion quite a different set of things and beings even on
this our plane, including in it all our planets. How
much more different then must be *external* nature in
other Solar systems, and how foolish is it to judge of
other *stars* and worlds and human beings by our own,
as physical science does!

ENQ. But what are your data for this assertion?

THEO. What science in general will never accept as proof —
the cumulative testimony of an endless series of Seers
who have testified to this fact. Their spiritual visions,
real explorations by, and through, physical and spiritual
senses untrammelled by blind flesh, were systematically
checked and compared one with the other, and their
nature sifted. All that was not corroborated by unani-
mous and collective experience was rejected, while that

only was recorded as established truth which, in various ages, under different climes, and throughout an un-
told series of incessant observations, was found to agree
and receive constantly further corroboration. The methods used by our scholars and students of the psycho-
spiritual sciences do not differ from those of students
of the natural and physical sciences, as you may see.
Only our fields of research are on two different planes,
and our instruments are made by no human hands, for
which reason perchance they are only the more reliable.
The retorts, accumulators, and microscopes of the chem-
ist and naturalist may get out of order; the telescope and
the astronomer's horological instruments may get
spoiled; our recording instruments are beyond the influence of weather or the elements.

ENQ. And therefore you have implicit faith in them?

THEO. Faith is a word not to be found in theosophical dic-
tionaries: we say *knowledge based on observation and
experience.* There is this difference, however, that
while the observation and experience of physical science lead the scientists to about as many "working" hypotheses as there are minds to evolve them, our *knowledge* consents to add to its lore only those facts which
have become undeniable, and which are fully and absolutely demonstrated.

ON THE SEPTENARY CONSTITUTION OF OUR PLANET

ENQ. I understand that you describe our earth as forming
part of a chain of earths?

THEO. We do. But the other six "earths" or globes, are not
on the same plane of objectivity as our earth is; therefore we cannot see them.

ENQ. Is that on account of the great distance?

THEO. Not at all, for we see with our naked eye planets and
even stars at immediately greater distances; but it is owing to those six globes being outside our physical means

of perception, or plane of being. It is not only that their material density, weight, or fabric are entirely different from those of our earth and the other known planets; but they are (to us) on an entirely different *layer* of space, so to speak; a layer not to be perceived or felt by our physical senses. And when I say "layer," please do not allow your fancy to suggest to you layers like strata or beds laid one over the other, for this would only lead to another absurd misconception. What I mean by "layer" is that plane of infinite space which by its nature cannot fall under our ordinary waking perceptions, whether mental or physical; but which exists in nature outside of our normal mentality or consciousness, outside of our three dimensional space, and outside of our division of time. Each of the seven fundamental planes (or layers) in space has its own objectivity and subjectivity, its own space and time, its own consciousness and set of senses.

ENQ. What do you mean by a different set of senses?

THEO. We have a different set of senses in dream-life, have we not? We feel, talk, hear, see, taste and function in general on a different plane; the change of state of our consciousness being evidenced by the fact that a series of acts and events embracing years, as we think, pass ideally through our mind in one instant. Well, that extreme rapidity of our mental operations in dreams, and the perfect naturalness, for the time being, of all the other functions, show us that we are on quite another plane. Our philosophy teaches us that, as there are seven fundamental forces in nature, and seven planes of being, so there are seven states of consciousness in which man can live, think, remember and have his being.

ENQ. You do not accept then, the well-known explanations of biology and physiology to account for the dream state?

THEO. We do not. Believing in seven planes of Kosmic being and states of Consciousness, with regard to the Universe or the Macrocosm, we stop at the fourth plane, finding it impossible to go with any degree of certainty beyond. But with respect to the Microcosm, or man, we speculate freely on his seven states and principles.

ENQ. How do you explain these?

THEO. We find, first of all, two distinct beings in man; the spiritual and the physical, the man who thinks, and the man who records as much of these thoughts as he is able to assimilate. Therefore we divide him into two distinct natures; the upper or the spiritual being, composed of three "principles" or *aspects;* and the lower or the physical quaternary, composed of *four* — in all *seven*.

ˊ THE SEPTENARY NATURE OF MAN

ENQ. Is it what we call Spirit and Soul, and the man of flesh?

THEO. It is not. That is the old Platonic division. Plato was an Initiate, and therefore could not go into forbidden details; but he who is acquainted with the archaic doctrine finds the seven in Plato's various combinations of Soul and Spirit. He regarded man as constituted of two parts — one eternal, formed of the same essence as the Absoluteness, the other mortal and corruptible, deriving its constituent parts from the *minor* "created" Gods. Man is composed, he shows, of (1) a mortal body, (2) an immortal principle, and (3) a "separate mortal kind of Soul." It is that which we respectively call the physical man, the Spiritual Soul or Spirit, and the animal Soul (the *Nous* and *psyche*). This is the division adopted by Paul, another Initiate, who maintains that there is a psychical body which is sown in the corruptible (astral soul or body), and a *spiritual* body that is raised in incorruptible substance. Even *James* (iii, 15) corroborates the same by saying that the "wisdom" (of our lower soul) descendeth not from the above, but is terrestrial ("psychical," "demoniacal," *vide* Greek text); while the other is heavenly wisdom. Now so plain is it that Plato and even Pythagoras, while speaking but of three "principles," give them seven separate functions, in their various combinations, that if we contrast our teachings this will become quite plain. Let us take a cursory view of these seven aspects by drawing two tables.

THEOSOPHICAL DIVISION

	SANSKRIT TERMS	EXOTERIC MEANING	EXPLANATORY
LOWER QUATERNARY	(a) Rupa, or Sthulasarira.	(a) Physical body.	(a) Is the vehicle of all the other "principles" during life.
	(b) Prana.	(b) Life, or Vital principle.	(b) Necessary only to *a, c, d,* and the functions of the lower *Manas,* which embrace all those limited to the (*physical*) brain.
	(c) Linga-sarira.	(c) Astral body.	(c) The *Double,* the phantom body.
	(d) Kama-rupa.	(d) The seat of animal desires and passions.	(d) This is the centre of the animal man, where lies the line of demarcation which separates the mortal man from the immortal entity.
THE UPPER IMPERISHABLE TRIAD	(e) *Manas* — a dual principle in its functions.	(e) Mind, Intelligence: which is the higher human mind, whose light, or radiation links the MONAD, for the lifetime, to the mortal man.	(e) The future state and the Karmic destiny of man depend on whether Manas gravitates more downward to Kama rupa, the seat of the animal passions, or upwards to *Buddhi,* the Spiritual *Ego.* In the latter case, the higher consciousness of the individual Spiritual aspirations of *mind* (Manas), assimilating Buddhi, are absorbed by it and form the *Ego,* which goes into Devachanic bliss.
	(f) Buddhi.	(f) The Spiritual Soul.	(f) The vehicle of pure universal spirit.
	(g) Atma.	(g) Spirit.	(g) One with the Absolute, as its radiation.

THE DISTINCTION BETWEEN SOUL AND SPIRIT

ENQ. Do you really teach, as you are accused of doing, the annihilation of every personality?

THEO. We do not. But as this question of the duality — the *individuality* of the Divine Ego, and the *personality* of the human animal — involves that of the possibility of the real immortal Ego appearing in *seance rooms* as a "materialized spirit," which we deny, our opponents have started the nonsensical charge. The general and almost invariable rule is the merging of the personal into the individual or immortal consciousness of the Ego, a transformation or a divine transfiguration, and the entire annihilation only of the lower *quaternary*. Would you expect the man of flesh, or the *temporary personality*, his shadow, the "astral," his animal instincts and even physical life, to survive with the "spiritual EGO" and become sempiternal? Naturally all this ceases to exist, either at, or soon after corporeal death. It becomes in time entirely disintegrated and disappears from view, being annihilated as a whole.

ENQ. Then you also reject *resurrection in the flesh?*

THEO. Most decidedly we do. Why should we, who believe in the archaic esoteric philosophy of the Ancients, accept the unphilosophical speculations of the later Christian theology, borrowed from the Egyptian and Greek exoteric systems of the Gnostics?

ENQ. The Egyptians revered Nature-Spirits, and deified even onions: your Hindus are *idolaters,* to this day; the Zoroastrians worshipped, and do still worship, the Sun; and the best Greek philosophers were either dreamers or materialists — witness Plato and Democritus. How can you compare!

THEO. It may be so in your modern Christian and even scientific catechism; it is not so for unbiased minds. The Egyptians revered the "One-Only-One," as *Nut;* and it is from this word that Anaxagoras got his denomination *Nous,* or as he calls it, Νους αὐτοκρατής, "the Mind or Spirit Self-potent," the ἀρχὴ τῆς κινήσεως, the leading motor, or *primum mobile* of all. With him the *Nous* was God, and the logos was man, his emanation. The *Nous* is the spirit (whether in Kosmos or in man), and the *logos,* whether Universe or astral body, the emanation of the former, the physical body being merely the animal. Our external powers perceive *phenomena*; our *Nous* alone is able to recognize their *noumena.* It is the logos alone, or the *noumenon,* that survives, because it is immortal in its very nature and essence, and the *logos* in man is the Eternal EGO, that which reincarnates and lasts for ever. But how can the evanescent or external shadow, the temporary clothing of that divine Emanation which returns to the source whence it proceeded, be that *which is raised in incorruptibility?*

ENQ. Still you can hardly escape the charge of having invented a new division of man's spiritual and psychic constituents; for no philosopher speaks of them, though you believe that Plato does.

THEO. And I support the view. Besides Plato, there is Pythagoras, who also followed the same idea.* He described the *Soul* as a self-moving Unit *(monad)* composed of three elements, the *Nous* (Spirit), the *phren* (mind), and the *thumos* (life, breath or the *Nephesh* of the Kabalists) which three correspond to our "Atma-Buddhi" (higher Spirit-Soul), to *Manas* (the EGO), and to *Kamarupa* in conjunction with the *lower* reflection of Manas. That which the Ancient Greek philosophers termed Soul, in general, we call Spirit, or Spiritual *Soul, Buddhi,* as the vehicle of *Atma* (the *Agathon,* or Plato's Supreme Deity). The fact that Pythagoras and others state

---

* "Plato and Pythagoras," say Plutarch, "distribute the soul into two parts, the rational (noetic) and irrational (agnoia); that that part of the soul of man which is rational is eternal; for though it be not God, yet it is the product of an eternal deity, but that part of the soul which is divested of reason (agnoia) dies." [*De placitio philosophorum,* Bk. IV, iv, vii.]

that *phren* and *thumos* are shared by us with the brutes proves that in this case the *lower* Manasic reflection (instinct) and *Kama-rupa* (animal living passions) are meant. And as Socrates and Plato accepted the clue and followed it, if to these five, namely, *Agathon* (Diety or Atma), *Psyche* (Soul in its collective sense), *Nous* (Spirit or Mind), *Phren* (physical mind), and *Thumos* (Kama-rupa or passions) we add the *eidolon* of the Mysteries, the shadowy *form* or the human double, and the *physical body*, it will be easy to demonstrate that the ideas of both Pythagoras and Plato were identical with ours. Even the Egyptians held to the Septenary division. In its exit, they taught, the Soul (EGO) had to pass through its seven chambers, or principles, those it left behind, and those it took along with itself. The only difference is that, ever bearing in mind the penalty of revealing Mystery-doctrines, which was *death,* they gave out the teaching in a broad outline, while we elaborate it and explain it in its details.

VII

ON THE VARIOUS POST-MORTEM STATES

THE PHYSICAL AND THE SPIRITUAL MAN

ENQ. I am glad to hear you believe in the immortality of the Soul.

THEO. Not of "the Soul," but of the divine Spirit; or rather in the immortality of the reincarnating Ego.

ENQ. What is the difference?

THEO. A very great one in our philosophy, but this is too abstruse and difficult a question to touch lightly upon. We shall have to analyse them separately, and then in conjunction. We may begin with Spirit.

We say that the Spirit (the "Father in secret" of Jesus), or *Atman,* is no individual property of any man, but is the Divine essence which has no body, no form, which is imponderable, invisible and indivisible, that which does not *exist* and yet *is,* as the Buddhists say of Nirvana. It only overshadows the mortal; that which enters into him and pervades the whole body being only its omnipresent rays, or light, radiated through *Buddhi,* its vehicle and direct emanation. This is the secret meaning of the assertions of almost all the ancient philosophers, when they said that "the *rational* part of man's soul"* never entered wholly into the man, but only overshadowed him more or less through the *irrational* spiritual Soul or *Buddhi.*†

---

* In its generic sense, the word "rational" meaning something emanating from the Eternal Wisdom.

† *Irrational* in the sense that as a *pure* emanation of the Universal mind it can have no individual reason of its own on this plane of matter, but like the Moon, who borrows her light from the Sun and her life from the Earth, so *Buddhi,* receiving its light of Wisdom from *Atma,* gets its rational qualities from *Manas. Per se,* as something homogeneous, it is devoid of attributes.

ENQ. I laboured under the impression that the "Animal Soul" alone was irrational, not the Divine.

THEO. You have to learn the difference between that which is negatively, or *passively* "irrational," because undifferentiated, and that which is irrational because too *active* and positive. Man is a correlation of spiritual powers, as well as a correlation of chemical and physical forces, brought into function by what we call "principles."

ENQ. I have read a good deal upon the subject, and it seems to me that the notions of the older philosophers differed a great deal from those of the mediaeval Kabalists, though they do agree in some particulars.

THEO. The most substantial difference between them and us is this. While we believe with the Neo-Platonists and the Eastern teachings that the spirit (Atma) never descends hypostatically into the living man, but only showers more or less its radiance on the *inner* man (the psychic and spiritual compound of the *astral* principles), the Kabalists maintain that the human Spirit, detaching itself from the ocean of light and Universal Spirit, enters man's Soul, where it remains throughout life imprisoned in the astral capsule.

ENQ. And what do you say?

THEO. We say that we only allow the presence of the radiation of Spirit (or Atma) in the astral capsule, and so far only as that spiritual radiancy is concerned. We say that man and Soul have to conquer their immortality by ascending towards the unity with which, if successful, they will be finally linked and into which they are finally, so to speak, absorbed. The individualization of man after death depends on the spirit, not on his soul and body. Although the word "personality," in the sense in which it is usually understood, is an absurdity if applied literally to our immortal essence, still the latter is, as our individual Ego, a distinct entity, immortal and eternal, *per se. It is only in the case of black magicians or of criminals beyond redemption, criminals who have been such during a long series of lives* — that the shining thread, which links the spirit to the *personal* soul from the moment of the birth of the child, is violently snapped, and the disembodied entity becomes divorced from the personal soul, the latter being annihilated without leaving the smallest impression of itself on the former. If that union between the lower, or personal Manas, and the individual reincarnating Ego has not been effected during life, then the former is left to share the fate of the lower animals, to gradually dissolve into ether, and have its personality annihilated. But even then the Ego remains a distinct being. It (the spiritual Ego) only loses one Devachanic state — after that special, and in that case indeed useless, life — as that idealized *Personality,* and is reincarnated, after enjoying for a short time its freedom as a planetary spirit, almost immediately.

ENQ. It is stated in *Isis Unveiled* that such planetary Spirits or Angels, "the gods of the Pagans or the Archangels of the Christians," will never be men on our planet.

THEO. Quite right. Not *"such,"* but *some* classes of higher Planetary Spirits. They will never be men on this planet, because they are liberated Spirits from a previous, earlier world, and as such they cannot rebecome men on this one. Yet all these will live again in the next and far higher Mahamanvantara, after this "great Age," and "Brahma *pralaya*" (a little period of 16 figures or so) is over. For you must have heard, of course, that Eastern philosophy teaches us that mankind consists of such "Spirits" imprisoned in human bodies? The difference between animals and men is this: the former are ensouled by the "principles" *potentially,* the latter *actually.* Do you understand now the difference?

ENQ. Yes; but this specialization has been in all ages the stumbling-block of metaphysicians.

THEO. It was. The whole esotericism of the Buddhistic philosophy is based on this mysterious teaching. Even metaphysicians are too inclined to confound the effect with the cause. An Ego who has won his immortal life as spirit will remain the same inner self throughout all his rebirths on earth; but this does not imply necessarily that he must either remain the Mr. Smith or Mr. Brown he was on earth, or lose his individuality. Therefore, the astral soul and the terrestrial body of man may, in the dark hereafter, be absorbed into the cosmical ocean of sublimated elements, and cease to feel his last *personal* Ego (if it did not deserve to soar higher) , and the *divine* Ego still remain the same unchanged entity, though this terrestrial experience of his emanation may be totally obliterated at the instant of separation from the unworthy vehicle.

ENQ. If the "Spirit," or the divine portion of the soul, is pre-existent as a distinct being from all eternity, as Origen, Synesius, and other philosophers taught, and if it is the same, and nothing more than the metaphysically-objective soul, how can it be otherwise than eternal? And what matters it in such a case whether man leads a pure life or an animal, if, do what he may, he can never lose his individuality?

THEO. This doctrine, as you have stated it, is just as pernicious in its consequences as that of vicarious atonement. Had the latter dogma, in company with the false idea that we are all immortal, been demonstrated to the world in its true light, humanity would have been bettered by its propagation.

Let me repeat to you again. Pythagoras, Plato, Timaeus of Locri, and the old Alexandrian School, derived the *Soul* of man (or his higher "principles" and attributes) from the Universal World Soul, the latter being, according to their teachings, *Aether* (Pater-Zeus) . Therefore, neither of these "principles" can be *unalloyed* essence of the Pythagorean *Monas,* or our *Atma-Buddhi,* because the *Anima Mundi* is but the effect,

the subjective emanation or rather radiation of the
former. Both the *human* Spirit (or the individuality),
the reincarnating Spiritual Ego, and Buddhi, the Spiritual soul, are pre-existent.

ENQ. Would you call the Soul, *i.e.,* the human thinking Soul,
or what you call the Ego — matter?

THEO. Not matter, but *substance* assuredly; nor would the
word "matter," if prefixed with the adjective, *primordial,* be a word to avoid. That matter, we say, is co-
eternal with Spirit, and is not our visible, tangible, and
divisible matter, but its extreme sublimation. Pure
Spirit is but one remove from the *no*-Spirit, or the absolute *all.* Unless you admit that man was evolved out of
this primordial Spirit-matter, and represents a regular
progressive scale of "principles" from *meta*-Spirit down
to the grossest matter, how can we ever come to regard
the *inner* man as immortal, and at the same time as a
spiritual Entity and a mortal man?

ENQ. Then why should you not believe in God as such an
Entity?

THEO. Because that which is infinite and unconditioned can
have no form, and cannot be a being. An "entity" is
immortal, but is so only in its ultimate essence, not in
its individual form. When at the last point of its cycle
it is absorbed into its primordial nature; and it becomes
spirit, when it loses its name of Entity.

Its immortality as a form is limited only to its life-
cycle or the *Mahamanvantara;* after which it is one and
identical with the Universal Spirit, and no longer a
separate Entity. As to the *personal* Soul — by which we
mean the spark of consciousness that preserves in the
Spiritual Ego the idea of the personal "I" of the last
incarnation — this lasts, as a separate distinct recollection, only throughout the Devachanic period; after
which time it is added to the series of other innumera-
ble incarnations of the Ego, like the remembrance in
our memory of one of a series of days, at the end of a

year. Will you bind the infinitude you claim for your God to finite conditions? That alone which is indissolubly cemented by *Atma* (*i.e.,* Buddhi-Manas) is immortal. The Soul of man (*i.e.,* of the personality) *per se* is neither immortal, eternal nor divine. Says the *Zohar* (I, 65 *c,* 66 *a*) , "just as the soul, when sent to this earth, puts on an earthly garment, to preserve herself here, so she receives above a shining garment, in order to be able to look without injury into the mirror, whose light proceeds from the Lord of Light." Moreover, the *Zohar* teaches that the soul cannot reach the abode of bliss unless she has received the "holy kiss," or the reunion of the soul *with the substance from which she emanated* — spirit.* All souls are dual, and, while the latter is a feminine principle, the spirit is masculine. While imprisoned in body, man is a trinity, unless his pollution is such as to have caused his divorce from the spirit. "Woe to the soul which prefers to her divine husband (spirit) the earthly wedlock with her terrestrial body," records a text of the *Book of the Keys,* a Hermetic work. Woe indeed, for nothing will remain of that personality to be recorded on the imperishable tablets of the Ego's memory.

ENQ. How can that which, if not breathed by God into man, yet is on your own confession of an identical substance with the divine, fail to be immortal?

THEO. Every atom and speck of matter, not of substance only, is *imperishable* in its essence, but not in its *individual consciousness.* Immortality is but one's unbroken consciousness; and the *personal* consciousness can hardly last longer than the personality itself, can it? And such consciousness survives only throughout Devachan, after which it is reabsorbed, first, in the *individual,* and then in the *universal* consciousness.

---

* [II, 97 *a*; I, 168 *a*.]

ON ETERNAL REWARD AND PUNISHMENT;
AND ON NIRVANA

ENQ. It is hardly necessary, I suppose, to ask you whether you believe in the Christian dogmas of Paradise and Hell, or in future rewards and punishments as taught by the Orthodox churches?

THEO. As described in your catechisms, we reject them absolutely; least of all would we accept their eternity. But we believe firmly in what we call the *Law of Retribution,* and in the absolute justice and wisdom guiding this Law, or Karma. Hence we positively refuse to accept the cruel and unphilosophical belief in eternal reward or eternal punishment.

ENQ. Have you any other reasons for rejecting this dogma?

THEO. Our chief reason for it lies in the fact of reincarnation. As already stated, we reject the idea of a new soul created for every newly-born babe. We believe that every human being is the bearer, or *Vehicle,* of an *Ego* coeval with every other Ego; because all *Egos* are *of the same essence* and belong to the primeval emanation from one universal infinite *Ego.* Plato calls the latter the *logos* (or the second manifested God) ; and we, the manifested divine principle, which is one with the universal mind or soul, not the anthropomorphic, extra-cosmic and *personal* God in which so many Theists believe.

ENQ. But where is the difficulty, once you accept a manifested principle, in believing that the soul of every new mortal is *created* by that Principle, as all the Souls before it have been so created?

THEO. Because that which is *impersonal* can hardly create, plan and think, at its own sweet will and pleasure. Being a universal *Law,* immutable in its periodical manifestations, those of radiating and manifesting its own essence at the beginning of every new cycle of life, IT is not supposed to create men, only to repent a few years later of having created them. If we have to believe in a divine principle at all, it must be in one which is as absolute harmony, logic, and justice as it is absolute love, wisdom, and impartiality; and a God who would *create* every soul for the space of *one brief span of life,* regardless of the fact whether it has to animate the body of a wealthy, happy man, or that of a poor suffering wretch, hapless from birth to death though he has done nothing to deserve his cruel fate — would be rather a senseless fiend than a God. Why, even the Jewish philosophers, believers in the Mosaic Bible (esoterically, of course), have never entertained such an idea; and, moreover, they believed in reincarnation, as we do.

ENQ. Can you give me some instances as a proof of this?

THEO. Most decidedly I can. Philo Judaeus says (in *De Somniis,* I, § 22) : "The air is full of them [of souls]; those which are nearest the earth, descending to be tied to mortal bodies, παλινδρομοῦσιν αὖθις, *return to other bodies, being desirous to live in them."* In the *Zohar,* the soul is made to plead her freedom before God: "Lord of the Universe! I am happy in this world, and do not wish to go into another world, where I shall be a bondmaid, and be exposed to all kinds of pollutions."* The doctrine of fatal necessity, the everlasting immutable law, is asserted in the answer of the Deity: "Against thy will thou becomest an embryo, and against thy will thou art born."† Light would be incomprehensible without darkness to make it manifest by contrast; good would be no longer good without evil to show the priceless nature of the boon; and so personal virtue could claim no merit unless it had passed through the furnace of temptation. Nothing is eternal and unchangeable, save the Concealed Deity. Nothing that is finite — whether because it had a beginning, or must have an end — can remain stationary. It must either progress or

---

* *Zohar,* II, 96 *a.* Amst. ed.
† *Mishnah Pirke Aboth,* IV, § 29.

recede; and a soul which thirsts after a reunion with its spirit, which alone confers upon it immortality, must purify itself through cyclic transmigrations onward towards the only land of bliss and eternal rest, called in the *Zohar,* "The Palace of Love," היכל אהבה;* in the Hindu religion, "Moksha"; among the Gnostics, "The Pleroma of Eternal Light"; and by the Buddhists, "Nirvana." And all these states are temporary, not eternal.

ENQ. Yet there is no reincarnation spoken of in all this.

THEO. A soul which pleads to be allowed to remain where she is, *must be pre-existent,* and not have been created for the occasion. In the *Zohar* (III, 61 *c*), however, there is a still better proof. Speaking of the reincarnating *Egos* (the *rational* souls), those whose last personality has to fade out *entirely,* it is said: "All souls which have alienated themselves in heaven from the Holy One — blessed be his Name — have thrown themselves into an abyss at their very existence, and have anticipated the time when they are to descend once more on earth." "The Holy One" means here, esoterically, the Atman, or *Atma-Buddhi.*

ENQ. Moreover, it is very strange to find *Nirvana* spoken of as something synonymous with the Kingdom of Heaven, or Paradise, since according to every Orientalist of note Nirvana is a synonym of annihilation!

THEO. Taken literally, with regard to the personality and differentiated matter, not otherwise. These ideas on reincarnation and the trinity of man were held by many of the early Christian Fathers. The personal soul must, of course, be disintegrated into its particles, before it is able to link its purer essence for ever with the immortal spirit. In Buddhistic philosophy *annihilation* means only a dispersion of matter, in whatever form or *semblance* of form it may be, for everything that has form is temporary, and is, therefore, really an illusion. For in eternity the longest periods of time

* [II, 97 *a*.]

are as a wink of the eye. So with form. Before we have
time to realize that we have seen it, it is gone like an instantaneous flash of lightning, and passed for ever.
When the Spiritual, *entity* breaks loose for ever from
every particle of matter, substance, or form, and rebecomes a Spiritual breath: then only does it enter upon
the eternal and unchangeable *Nirvana,* lasting as long
as the cycle of life has lasted — an eternity, truly. And
then that Breath, existing *in Spirit,* is *nothing* because
it is *all;* as a form, a semblance, a shape, it is completely
annihilated; as absolute Spirit it still *is,* for it has become *Be-ness* itself. The very word used, "absorbed in
the universal essence," when spoken of the "Soul" as
Spirit, means *"union with."* It can never mean annihilation, as that would mean eternal separation.

ENQ. Do you not lay yourself open to the accusation of
preaching annihilation by the language you yourself
use? You have just spoken of the Soul of man returning
to its primordial elements.

THEO. But you forget that I have given you the differences
between the various meanings of the word "Soul," and
shown the loose way in which the term "Spirit" has been
hitherto translated. We speak of an *animal,* a *human,*
and a *spiritual,* Soul, and distinguish between them.
Plato, for instance, calls "rational SOUL" that which we
call *Buddhi,* adding to it the adjective of "spiritual,"
however; but that which we call the reincarnating Ego,
Manas, he calls Spirit, *Nous,* etc., whereas we apply the
term *Spirit,* when standing alone and without any qualification, to Atma alone. Pythagoras repeats our doctrine when stating that the *Ego* (*Nous*) is eternal with
Deity; that the soul only passed through various stages
to arrive at divine excellence; while *thumos* returned
to the earth, and even the *phren,* the lower *Manas,* was
eliminated. Again, Plato defines *Soul* (Buddhi) as "the
motion that is able to move itself." "Soul," he adds,
"is the most ancient of all things, and the commence-
ment of motion," thus calling Atma-Buddhi "Soul,"

and *Manas* "Spirit," which we do not.

"Soul was generated prior to body, and body is posterior
and secondary, as being according to nature, ruled over by
the ruling soul." "The soul which administers all things
that are moved in every way, administers likewise the
heavens."

"Soul then leads everything in heaven, and on earth, and
in the sea, by its movement — the names of which are, to
will, to consider, to take care of, to consult, to form opinions
true and false, to be in a state of joy, sorrow, confidence,
fear, hate, love, together with all such primary movements
as are allied to these. . . . Being a goddess herself, she ever
takes as an ally *Nous,* a god, and disciplines all things correctly and happily; but when with *Anoia* — not *nous* — it
works out everything the contrary."*

In this language, as in the Buddhist texts, the negative
is treated as essential existence. *Annihilation* comes under a similar exegesis. The positive state is essential
being, but no manifestation as such. When the spirit,
in Buddhistic parlance, enters *Nirvana,* it loses objective existence, but retains subjective being. To objective minds this is becoming absolute "nothing"; to
subjective, NO-THING, nothing to be displayed to sense.
Thus, their Nirvana means the certitude of individual
immortality *in Spirit,* not in Soul, which, though "the
most ancient of all things," is still — along with all the
other *Gods* — a finite emanation, in *forms* and individuality, if not in substance.

ON THE VARIOUS PRINCIPLES IN MAN

ENQ. I have heard a good deal about this constitution of the
"inner man" as you call it, but could never make "head
or tail on't" as Gabalis expresses it.

THEO. Of course, it is most difficult, and, as you say, puz-
zling to understand correctly and distinguish between

---

* *The Laws,* X, 896-7 B.

the various *aspects,* called by us the "principles" of the
real Ego. It is the more so as there exists a notable difference in the numbering of those principles by various
Eastern schools, though at the bottom there is the same
identical substratum of teaching.

ENQ. Do you mean the Vedantins, as an instance? Don't they
divide your seven "principles" into five only?

THEO. They do; but though I would not presume to dispute
the point with a learned Vedantin, I may yet state as my
private opinion that they have an obvious reason for it.
With them it is only that compound spiritual aggregate
which consists of various mental aspects that is called
Man at all, the physical body being in their view something beneath contempt, and merely an *illusion.* Nor
is the Vedanta the only philosophy to reckon in this
manner. Lao-Tze, in his *Tao-te-King,* mentions only
five principles, because he, like the Vedantins, omits to
include two principles, namely, the spirit (Atma) and
the physical body, the latter of which, moreover, he calls
"the cadaver." Then there is the *Taraka Raja Yoga*
School. Its teaching recognizes only three "principles"
in fact; but then, in reality, their *Sthulopadhi,* or the
physical body, in its waking conscious state, their
Sukshmopadhi, the same body in *Svapna,* or the dream-
ing state, and their *Karanopadhi* or "causal body," or
that which passes from one incarnation to another, are
all dual in their aspects, and thus make six. Add to this
Atma, the impersonal divine principle or the immortal
element in Man, undistinguished from the Universal
Spirit, and you have the same seven again.*

ENQ. Then it seems almost the same as the division made by
the mystic Christians: body, soul and spirit?

THEO. Just the same. We could easily make of the body the
vehicle of the "vital Double"; of the latter the vehicle
of Life or *Prana;* of *Kama-rupa,* or (animal) soul, the

---

* See *The Secret Doctrine* for a clearer explanation. Vol. I, p. 157. [p 209
Adyar Ed.]

vehicle of the *higher* and the *lower* mind, and make of this six principles, crowning the whole with the one immortal spirit. In Occultism every qualificative change in the state of our consciousness gives to man a new aspect, and if it prevails and becomes part of the living and acting Ego, it must be (and is) given a special name, to distinguish the man in that particular state from the man he is when he places himself in another state.

ENQ. It is just that which it is so difficult to understand.

THEO. It seems to me very easy, on the contrary, once that you have seized the main idea, *i.e.,* that man acts on this or another plane of consciousness, in strict accordance with his mental and spiritual condition. Divide the terrestrial being called man into three chief aspects, if you like, and unless you make of him a pure animal you cannot do less. Take his objective *body;* the thinking principle in him — which is only a little higher than the *instinctual* element in the animal — or the vital conscious soul; and that which places him so immeasurably beyond and higher than the animal — *i.e.,* his *reasoning* soul or "spirit." Well, if we take these three groups or representative entities, and subdivide them, according to the occult teaching, what do we get?

First of all, Spirit (in the sense of the Absolute, and therefore, indivisible ALL) , or Atma. As this can neither be located nor limited in philosophy, being simply that which is in Eternity, and which cannot be absent from even the tiniest geometrical or mathematical point of the universe of matter or substance, it ought not to be called, in truth, a "human" principle at all. Rather, and at best, it is in Metaphysics that point in space which the human Monad and its vehicle man occupy for the period of every life. Now that point is as imaginary as man himself, and in reality is an illusion, a *maya;* but then for ourselves, as for other personal Egos, we are a reality during that fit of illusion called life, and we have to take ourselves into account, in our own fancy at any rate, if no one else does. To make it more conceivable to the human intellect, when first attempting the study of Occultism, and to solve the A B C of the mystery of man, Occultism calls this *seventh* principle the synthesis of the sixth, and gives it for vehicle the *Spiritual* Soul, *Buddhi.* Now the latter conceals a mystery, which is never given to any one, with the exception of irrevocably pledged *chelas,* or those, at any rate, who can be safely trusted. This divine soul, or Buddhi, then, is the vehicle of the Spirit. In conjunction, these two are one, impersonal and without any attributes (on this plane, of course), and make two spiritual principles. If we pass on to the *Human* Soul, *Manas* or *mens,* every one will agree that the intelligence of man is *dual* to say the least: *e.g.,* the high-minded man can hardly become low-minded; the very intellectual and spiritual-minded man is separated by an abyss from the obtuse, dull, and material, if not animal-minded man.

ENQ. But why should not man be represented by two principles or two aspects, rather?

THEO. Every man has these two principles in him, one more active than the other, and in rare cases one of these is entirely stunted in its growth, so to say, or paralysed by the strength and predominance of the other *aspect,* in whatever direction. These, then, are what we call the two principles or aspects of *Manas,* the higher and the lower; the former, the higher Manas, or the thinking, conscious EGO gravitating towards the spiritual Soul (Buddhi); and the latter, or its instinctual principle, attracted to *Kama,* the seat of animal desires and passions in man. Thus, we have *four* principles justified; the last three being (1) the "Double," which we have agreed to call Protean, or Plastic Soul; the vehicle of (2) the life *principle;* and (3) the physical body.

ENQ. But what is it that reincarnates, in your belief?

THEO. The Spiritual thinking Ego, the permanent principle in man, or that which is the seat of *Manas.* It is not

Atma, or even Atma-Buddhi, regarded as the dual *Monad,* which is the *individual,* or *divine* man, but Manas; for Atman is the Universal ALL, and becomes the HIGHER-SELF of man only in conjunction with *Buddhi,* its vehicle, which links IT to the individuality (or divine man). For it is the Buddhi-Manas which is called the *Causal body* (the United 5th and 6th Principles), and which is *Consciousness* that connects it with every personality it inhabits on earth. Therefore, Soul being a generic term, there are in men three *aspects* of Soul — the terrestrial, or animal; the Human Soul; and the Spiritual Soul; these, strictly speaking, are one Soul in its three aspects. Now of the first aspect, nothing remains after death; of the second (*nous* or Manas) only its divine essence *if left unsoiled* survives, while the third in addition to being immortal becomes *consciously* divine, by the assimilation of the higher Manas. But to make it clear, we have to say a few words first of all about Reincarnation.

VIII

ON REINCARNATION OR REBIRTH

WHAT IS MEMORY ACCORDING TO THEOSOPHICAL TEACHING?

ENQ. The most difficult thing for you to do will be to explain and give reasonable grounds for such a belief. No Theosophist has ever yet succeeded in bringing forward a single valid proof to shake my scepticism.

THEO. Your argument tends to the same old objection; the loss of memory in each of us of our previous incarnation. You think it invalidates our doctrine? My answer is that it does not, and that at any rate such an objection cannot be final.

ENQ. I would like to hear your arguments.

THEO. They are short and few. Yet when you take into consideration (a) the utter inability of the best modern psychologists to explain to the world the nature of *mind;* and (b) their complete ignorance of its potentialities, and higher states, you have to admit that this objection is based on an *a priori* conclusion drawn from *prima facie* and circumstantial evidence more than anything else. Now what is "memory" in your conception, pray?

ENQ. That which is generally accepted: the faculty in our mind of remembering and of retaining the knowledge of previous thoughts, deeds and events.

THEO. Please add to it that there is a great difference between the three accepted forms of memory. Besides memory in general you have *Remembrance, Recollection* and *Reminiscence,* have you not? Have you ever thought over the difference? Memory, remember, is a generic name.

ENQ. Yet, all these are only synonyms.

THEO. Indeed, they are not — not in philosophy, at all events. Memory is simply an innate power in thinking beings, and even in animals, of reproducing past impressions by an association of ideas principally suggested by objective things or by some action on our external sensory organs. Memory is a faculty depending entirely on the more or less healthy and normal functioning of our *physical* brain; and *remembrance* and *recollection* are the attributes and handmaidens of that memory. But *reminiscence* is an entirely different thing. Reminiscence is defined as something intermediate between *remembrance* and *recollection,* or "a conscious process of recalling past occurrences, but *without that full and varied reference* to particular things which characterize *recollection.*" Locke, speaking of recollection and remembrance, says: "When an *idea again* recurs without the operation of the like object on the external sensory, it is *remembrance;* if it be sought after by the mind, and with pain and endeavour found and brought again into view, it is *recollection.*" But even Locke leaves *reminiscence* without any clear definition, because it is no faculty or attribute of our *physical* memory, but an intuitional perception apart from and outside our physical brain; a perception which, covering as it does (being called into action by the ever-present knowledge of our spiritual Ego) all those visions in man which are regarded as *abnormal* — from the pictures suggested by genius to the *ravings* of fever and even madness — are classed by science as having no *existence* outside of our fancy. Occultism and Theosophy, however, regard *reminiscence* in an entirely different light. For us, while *memory* is physical and evanescent and depends on the physiological conditions of the brain we call *reminiscence* the *memory of the soul.* And it is *this* memory which gives the assurance to almost every human being, whether he understands it or not, of his having lived before and having to live again. Indeed, as Wordsworth has it:

> Our birth is but a sleep and a forgetting,
>   The soul that rises with us, our life's Star,
> Hath had elsewhere its setting,
>   And cometh from afar.*

ENQ. If it is on this kind of memory — poetry and abnormal fancies, on your own confession — that you base your doctrine, then you will convince very few, I am afraid.

THEO. I did not "confess" it was a fancy. I simply said that physiologists and scientists in general regard such reminiscences as hallucinations and fancy, to which *learned* conclusion they are welcome. We do not deny that such visions of the past and glimpses far back into the corridors of time are not abnormal, as contrasted with our normal daily life experience and physical memory. Besides which we maintain that memory, as Olympiodorus called it, is simply *phantasy,* and the most unreliable thing in us.† Ammonius Saccas asserted that the only faculty in man directly opposed to prognostication, or looking into futurity, is *memory.* Furthermore, remember that memory is one thing and mind or *thought* is another; one is a recording machine, a register which very easily gets out of order; the other (thoughts) are eternal and imperishable. Would you refuse to believe in the existence of certain things or men only because your physical eyes have not seen them? Would not the collective testimony of past generations who have seen

---

* ["Ode on Intimations of Immortality."]
† "The phantasy," says Olympiodorus (*Comm. on the Phaedo*), "is an impediment to our intellectual conceptions; and hence, when we are agitated by the inspiring influence of the Divinity, if the phantasy intervenes, the enthusiastic energy ceases: for enthusiasm and the ecstasy are contrary to each other. Should it be asked whether the soul is able to energize without the phantasy, we reply, that its perception of universals proves that it is able. It has perceptions, therefore, independent of the phantasy; at the same time, however, the phantasy attends in its energies, just as a storm pursues him who sails on the sea."

him be a sufficient guarantee that Julius Caesar once lived? Why should not the same testimony of the psychic senses of the masses be taken into consideration?

ENQ. But don't you think that these are too fine distinctions to be accepted by the majority of mortals?

THEO. Say rather by the majority of materialists. And to them we say, behold: even in the short span of ordinary existence, memory is too weak to register all the events of a lifetime. How frequently do even most important events lie dormant in our memory until awakened by some association of ideas, or aroused to function and activity by some other link. This is especially the case with people of advanced age, who are always found suffering from feebleness of recollection. When, therefore, we remember that which we know about the physical and the spiritual principles in man, it is not the fact that our memory has failed to record our precedent life and lives that ought to surprise us, but the contrary, were it to happen.

WHY DO WE NOT REMEMBER OUR PAST LIVES?

ENQ. You have given me a bird's eye view of the seven principles; now how do they account for our complete loss of any recollection of having lived before?

THEO. Very easily. Since those principles which we call physical, and none of which is denied by science, though it calls them by other names,* are disintegrated after death with their constituent elements, *memory* along with its brain, this vanished memory of a vanished personality can neither remember nor record anything in the subsequent reincarnation of the EGO. Reincarnation means that this Ego will be furnished with a *new* body, a *new* brain, and a *new* memory. Therefore it would

_____
* Namely, the body, life, passional and animal instincts, and the astral eidolon of every man (whether perceived in thought or our mind's eye, or objectively and separate from the physical body), which principles we call *Sthula-Sarira, Prana, Kama-rupa,* and *Linga-sarira* (*vide supra*).

be as absurd to expect this *memory* to remember that which it has never recorded as it would be idle to examine under a microscope a shirt never worn by a murderer, and seek on it for the stains of blood which are to be found only on the clothes he wore. It is not the clean shirt that we have to question, but the clothes worn during the perpetration of the crime; and if these are burnt and destroyed, how can you get at them?

ENQ. Aye! how can you get at the certainty that the crime was ever committed at all, or that the "man in the clean shirt" ever lived before?

THEO. Not by physical processes, most assuredly; nor by relying on the testimony of that which exists no longer. But there is such a thing as circumstantial evidence, since our wise laws accept it, more, perhaps, even than they should. To get convinced of the fact of reincarnation and past lives, one must put oneself in *rapport* with one's real permanent Ego, not one's evanescent memory.

ENQ. But how can people believe in that which they *do not know,* nor have ever seen, far less put themselves in *rapport* with it?

THEO. If people will believe in the Gravity, Ether, Force, and what not of science, abstractions "and working hypotheses," which they have neither seen, touched, smelt, heard, nor tasted — why should not other people believe, on the same principle, in one's permanent Ego, a far more logical and important "working hypothesis" than any other?

ENQ. What is, finally, this mysterious eternal principle? Can you explain its nature so as to make it comprehensible to all?

THEO. The EGO which reincarnates, the *individual* and immortal — not personal — "I"; the vehicle, in short, of the Atma-Buddhic MONAD, that which is rewarded in Devachan and punished on earth, and that, finally, to which the reflection only of the *Skandhas,* or attributes, of every incarnation attaches itself.*

ENQ. What do you mean by *Skandhas?*

THEO. Just what I said: "attributes," among which is *memory,* all of which perish like a flower, leaving behind them only a feeble perfume. Here is another paragraph from H. S. Olcott's *The Buddhist Catechism*† which bears directly upon the subject. It deals with the question as follows: "The aged man remembers the incidents of his youth, despite his being physically and mentally changed. Why, then, is not the recollection of past lives brought over by us from our last birth into the present birth? Because memory is included within the Skandhas, and the Skandhas having changed with the new existence, a memory, the record of that particular existence, develops. Yet the record or reflection of all the past lives must survive, for when Prince Siddhartha became Buddha, the full sequence of his previous births were seen by him. . . . and any one who attains to the state of *Jhana* can thus retrospectively trace the line of his lives." This proves to you that while the undying qualities of the personality — such as love, goodness, charity, etc. — attach themselves to the immortal Ego, photographing on it, so to speak, a permanent image of the divine aspect of the man who was, his material Skandhas (those which generate the most marked Karmic effects) are as evanescent as a flash of lightning, and cannot impress the new brain of the new personality; yet their failing to do so impairs in no way the identity of the reincarnating Ego.

ENQ. Do you mean to infer that that which survives is only the Soul-memory, as you call it, that Soul or Ego being one and the same, while nothing of the personality remains?

---

* There are five *Skandhas* or attributes in the Buddhist teachings: "*Rupa* (form of body), material qualities; *Vedana,* sensation; *Sanna,* abstract ideas; *Sankhara,* tendencies of mind; *Vinnana,* mental powers. Of these we are formed; by them we are conscious of existence; and through them communicate with the world about us."

† By H. S. Olcott, President-Founder of the Theosophical Society.

THEO. Not quite; something of each personality, unless the latter was an *absolute* materialist with not even a chink in his nature for a spiritual ray to pass through, must survive, as it leaves its eternal impress on the incarnating permanent Self or Spiritual Ego.* (See "On *post mortem* and *post natal* Consciousness.") The personality with its Skandhas is ever changing with every new birth. It is, as said before, only the part played by the actor (the true Ego) for one night. This is why we preserve no memory on the physical plane of our past lives, though the *real* Ego has lived them over and knows them all.

ENQ. Then how does it happen that the real or Spiritual man does not impress his new personal "I" with this knowledge?

THEO. Because the Spiritual Ego can act only when the personal Ego is paralysed. The Spiritual "I" in man is omniscient and has every knowledge innate in it; while the personal self is the creature of its environment and the slave of the physical memory. Could the former manifest itself uninterruptedly, and without impediment, there would be no longer men on earth, but we should all be gods.

ENQ. Still there ought to be exceptions, and some ought to remember.

THEO. And so there are. But who believes in their report? Such sensitives are generally regarded as hallucinated hysteriacs, as crack-brained enthusiasts, or humbugs, by modern materialism. One speaks to people of soul, and some ask "What is Soul?" "Have you ever proved its existence?" Of course it is useless to argue with those who are materialists. But even to them I would put the question: "Can you remember what you were or did when a baby? Have you preserved the smallest recollection of your life, thoughts, or deeds, or that you lived

* Or the *Spiritual,* in contradistinction to the personal *Self.* The student must not confuse this Spiritual Ego with the "HIGHER SELF" which is *Atma,* the God within us, and inseparable from the Universal Spirit.

at all during the first eighteen months or two years of your existence? Then why not deny that you have ever lived as a babe, on the same principle?" When to all this we add that the reincarnating Ego, or *individuality,* retains during the Devachanic period merely the essence of the experience of its past earth-life or personality, the whole physical experience involving into a state of *in potentia,* or being, so to speak, translated into spiritual formulae; when we remember further that the term between two rebirths is said to extend from ten to fifteen centuries, during which time the physical consciousness is totally and absolutely inactive, having no organs to act through, and therefore *no existence,* the reason for the absence of all remembrance in the purely physical memory is apparent.

ENQ. You just said that the SPIRITUAL EGO was omniscient. Where, then, is that vaunted omniscience during his Devachanic life, as you call it?

THEO. During that time it is latent and potential, because, first of all, the Spiritual Ego (the compound of Buddhi-Manas) is *not* the Higher SELF, which being one with the Universal Soul or Mind is alone omniscient; and, secondly, because Devachan is the idealized continuation of the terrestrial life just left behind, a period of retributive adjustment, and a reward for unmerited wrongs and sufferings undergone in that special life. It is omniscient only *potentially* in Devachan, and *de facto* exclusively in Nirvana, when the Ego is merged in the Universal Mind-Soul. Yet it rebecomes *quasi* omniscient during those hours on earth when certain abnormal conditions and physiological changes in the body make the *Ego* free from the trammels of matter.

ON INDIVIDUALITY AND PERSONALITY

ENQ. But what is the difference between the two?

THEO. To understand the idea well, you have to first study the dual sets of principles: the *spiritual,* or those which belong to the imperishable Ego; and the *material,* or those principles which make up the ever-changing bodies or the series of personalities of that Ego. Let us fix names to these, and say that:

I. *Atma,* the *"Higher Self,"* is neither your Spirit nor mine, but like sunlight shines on all. It is the universally diffused *"divine principle,"* and is inseparable from its one and absolute *Meta*-Spirit, as the sunbeam is inseparable from sunlight.

II. *Buddhi* (the spiritual soul) is only its vehicle. Neither each separately, nor the two collectively, are of any more use to the body of man than sunlight and its beams are for a mass of granite buried in the earth, *unless the divine Duad is assimilated by, and reflected in,* some *consciousness.* Neither Atma nor Buddhi are ever reached by Karma, because the former is the highest aspect of Karma, *its working agent* of ITSELF in one aspect, and the other is unconscious *on this plane.* This consciousness or mind is,

III. *Manas,** the derivation or product in a reflected form of *Ahamkara,* "the conception of I," or EGO SHIP. It is, therefore, when inseparably united to the first two, called the SPIRITUAL EGO, and *Taijasa* (the radiant). This is the real Individuality, or the divine man. It is this Ego which — having originally incarnated in the *senseless* human form animated by, but unconscious (since it had no consciousness) of, the presence in itself of the dual monad — made of that human-like form *a real man.* It is that Ego, that "Causal

---

* MAHAT or the "Universal Mind" is the source of Manas. The latter is Mahat, *i.e.,* mind, in man. Manas is also called *Kshetrajna,* "embodied Spirit," because it is, according to our philosophy, the *Manasa-putras,* or "Sons of the Universal Mind," who *created,* or rather produced, the *thinking* man, *"manu,"* by incarnating in the *third Race* mankind in our Round. It is Manas, therefore, which is the real incarnating and permanent *Spiritual Ego,* the INDIVIDUALITY, and our various and numberless personalities only its external masks.

Body," which overshadows every personality Karma forces it to incarnate into; and this Ego which is held responsible for all the sins committed through, and in, every new body or personality — the evanescent masks which hide the true Individual through the long series of rebirths.

ENQ. But is this just? Why should this Ego receive punishment as the result of deeds which it has forgotten?

THEO. It has not forgotten them; it knows and remembers its misdeeds as well as you remember what you have done yesterday. Is it because the memory of that bundle of physical compounds called "body" does not recollect what its predecessor (the personality *that was*) did, that you imagine that the real Ego has forgotten them?

ENQ. But are there no modes of communication between the Spiritual and human consciousness or memory?

THEO. Of course there are. To what do you attribute intuition, the "voice of conscience," premonitions, vague undefined reminiscences, etc., etc., if not to such communications? Would that the majority of educated men, at least, had the fine spiritual perceptions of Coleridge, who shows how intuitional he is in some of his comments. Hear what he says with respect to the probability that "all thoughts are in themselves imperishable." "If the intelligent faculty (sudden 'revivals' of memory) should be rendered more comprehensive, it would require only a different and appropriate organization, the *body celestial* instead of the *body terrestrial,* to bring before every human soul *the collective experience of its whole past existence* (*existences,* rather)." And this *body celestial* is our Manasic EGO.

ON THE REWARD AND PUNISHMENT OF THE EGO

ENQ. I have heard you say that the *Ego,* whatever the life of the person he incarnated in may have been on Earth, is never visited with *post-mortem* punishment.

THEO. Never, save in very exceptional and rare cases.

ENQ. But if it is punished in this life for the misdeeds committed in a previous one, then it is this Ego that ought to be rewarded also, whether here, or when disincarnated.

THEO. And so it is. If we do not admit of any punishment outside of this earth, it is because the only state the Spiritual Self knows of, hereafter, is that of unalloyed bliss.

ENQ. What do you mean?

THEO. Simply this: *crimes and sins committed on a plane of objectivity and in a world of matter, cannot receive punishment in a world of pure subjectivity.* We believe in no hell or paradise as localities; in no objective hell-fires and worms that never die, nor in any Jerusalems with streets paved with sapphires and diamonds. What we believe in is a *post-mortem state* or mental condition, such as we are in during a vivid dream. We believe in an immutable law of absolute Love, Justice, and Mercy. And believing in it, we say: "Whatever the sin and dire results of the original Karmic transgression of the now incarnated Egos* no man (or the outer material and periodical form of the Spiritual Entity) can be held, with any degree of justice, responsible for the conse-

---

* It is on this transgression that the cruel and illogical dogma of the Fallen Angels has been built. It is explained in Vol. IV, [Adyar Ed.] of *The Secret Doctrine.* All our "Egos" are thinking and rational entities (*Manasa-putras*) who had lived, whether under human or other forms, in the precedent *life-cycle* (Manvantara), and whose Karma it was to incarnate in the *man* of this one. It was taught in the MYSTERIES that, having delayed to comply with this law (or having "refused to create" as Hinduism says of the *Kumaras* and Christian legend of the Archangel Michael), *i.e.*, having failed to incarnate in due time, the bodies predestined for them got defiled (*Vide* Stanzas VIII and IX in the "Slokas of Dzyan," Vol. III, *The Secret Doctrine,* pp. 31 and 32), hence the original sin of the senseless forms and the punishment of the *Egos.* That which is meant by the rebellious angels being hurled down into Hell is simply explained by these pure Spirits or Egos being imprisoned in bodies of unclean matter, flesh.

quences of his birth. The same unerringly wise and just rather than merciful Law, which inflicts upon the incarnated Ego the Karmic punishment for every sin committed during the preceding life on Earth, provided for the now disembodied Entity a long lease of mental rest, *i.e.*, the entire oblivion of every sad event, aye, to the smallest painful thought, that took place in its last life as a personality, leaving in the soul-memory but the reminiscence of that which was bliss, or led to happiness. Plotinus, who said that our body was the true river of Lethe, for "souls plunged into it forget all," meant more than he said. For, as our terrestrial body is like Lethe, so is our *celestial body* in Devachan, and much more.

ENQ. Then am I to understand that the murderer, the transgressor of law divine and human in every shape, is allowed to go unpunished?

THEO. Who ever said that? Our philosophy has a doctrine of punishment as stern as that of the most rigid Calvinist, only far more philosophical and consistent with absolute justice. No deed, not even a sinful thought, will go unpunished; the latter more severely even than the former, as a thought is far more potential in creating evil results than even a deed. We believe in an unerring law of Retribution, called KARMA, which asserts itself in a natural concatenation of causes and their unavoidable results.

ENQ. And how, or where, does it act?

THEO. Every labourer is worthy of his hire, saith Wisdom in the Gospel; every action, good or bad, is a prolific parent, saith the Wisdom of the Ages. Put the two together, and you will find the "why." After allowing the Soul, escaped from the pangs of personal life, a sufficient, aye, a hundredfold compensation, Karma, with its army of Skandhas, waits at the threshold of Devachan, whence the *Ego* re-emerges to assume a new incarnation. It is at this moment that the future destiny of the now-rested Ego trembles in the scales of just Retribution, as *it* now falls once again under the sway of active Karmic law. It is in this rebirth which is ready for *it*, a rebirth selected and prepared by this mysterious, inexorable, but in the equity and wisdom of its decrees infallible LAW, that the sins of the previous life of the Ego are punished. Only it is into no imaginary Hell, with theatrical flames and ridiculous tailed and horned devils, that the Ego is cast, but verily on to this earth, the plane and region of his sins, where he will have to atone for every bad thought and deed. As he has sown, so will he reap. Reincarnation will gather around him all those other Egos who have suffered, whether directly or indirectly, at the hands, or even through the unconscious instrumentality, of the past *personality*. They will be thrown by Nemesis in the way of the *new* man, concealing the *old*, the eternal EGO, and . . .

ENQ. But where is the equity you speak of, since these *new* personalities are not aware of having sinned or been sinned against?

THEO. Has the coat torn to shreds from the back of the man who stole it, by another man who was robbed of it and recognizes his property, to be regarded as fairly dealt with? The new personality is no better than a fresh suit of clothes with its specific characteristics, colour, form and qualities; but the *real* man who wears it is the same culprit as of old. It is the *individuality* who suffers through his personality. And it is this, and this alone, that can account for the terrible, still only *apparent*, injustice in the distribution of lots in life to man. When your modern philosophers will have succeeded in showing to us a good reason why so many apparently innocent and good men are born only to suffer during a whole lifetime; why so many are born poor unto starvation in the slums of great cities, abandoned by fate and men; why, while these are born in the gutter, others open their eyes to light in palaces; while a noble birth and fortune seem often given to the worst of men and only rarely to the worthy; while there are beggars whose *inner* selves are peers to the highest and noblest of men; when this, and much more, is satisfactorily explained by either your philosophers or theologians, then only, but not till then, you will have the right to reject the theory of reincarnation.

IX

ON THE KAMA-LOKA AND DEVACHAN

ON THE FATE OF THE LOWER PRINCIPLES

ENQ. You spoke of *Kama-loka,* what is it?

THEO. When the man dies, his lower three principles leave him for ever; *i.e.,* body, life, and vehicle of the latter, the astral body or the double of the *living* man. And then, his four principles — the central or middle principle, the animal soul or *Kama-rupa,* with what it has assimilated from the lower Manas, and the higher triad find themselves in *Kama-loka.* The latter is an astral locality, the *limbus* of scholastic theology, the *Hades* of the ancients, and, strictly speaking, a *locality* only in a relative sense. It has neither a definite area nor boundary, but exists *within* subjective space; *i.e.,* is beyond our sensuous perceptions. Still it exists, and it is there that the astral *eidolons* of all the beings that have lived, animals included, await their *second death.* For the animals it comes with the disintegration and the entire fading out of their *astral* particles to the last. For the human *eidolon* it begins when the Atma-Buddhi-Manasic triad is said to "separate" itself from its lower principles, or the reflection of the *ex-personality,* by falling into the Devachanic state.

ENQ. And what happens after this?

THEO. Then the *Kama-rupic* phantom, remaining bereft of its informing thinking principle, the higher *Manas,* and the lower aspect of the latter, the animal intelligence, no longer receiving light from the higher mind, and no longer having a physical brain to work through, collapses.

ENQ. In what way?

THEO. It can think no more, even on the lowest animal plane. Henceforth it is no longer even the lower Manas, since this "lower" is nothing without the "higher."

ENQ. And is it *this* nonentity which we find materializing in Seance rooms with Mediums?

THEO. It is this nonentity. A true nonentity, however, only as to reasoning or cogitating powers, still an *Entity,* however astral and fluidic, as shown in certain cases when, having been magnetically and unconsciously drawn towards a medium, it is revived for a time and lives in him by *proxy,* so to speak. In the medium's Aura, it lives a kind of vicarious life and reasons and speaks either through the medium's brain or those of other persons present. But this would lead us too far, and upon other people's grounds, whereon I have no desire to trespass. Let us keep to the subject of reincarnation.

ENQ. What of the latter? How long does the incarnating *Ego* remain in the Devachanic state?

THEO. This, we are taught, depends on the degree of spirituality and the merit or demerit of the last incarnation. The average time is from ten to fifteen centuries.

ENQ. But why could not this Ego manifest and communicate with mortals as Spiritualists will have it? What is there to prevent a mother from communicating with the children she left on earth, a husband with his wife, and so on? It is a most consoling belief, I must confess; nor do I wonder that those who believe in it are so averse to give it up.

THEO. Nor are they forced to, unless they happen to prefer truth to fiction, however "consoling." Uncongenial our doctrines may be to Spiritualists; yet, nothing of what we believe in and teach is half as selfish and cruel as what they preach.

ENQ. I do not understand you. What is selfish?

THEO. Their doctrine of the return of Spirits, the real "personalities" as they say; and I will tell you why. If *Devachan* — call it paradise if you like, a "place of bliss and of supreme felicity," if it is anything — is such a place (or say *state*), logic tells us that no sorrow or even a shade of pain can be experienced therein. "God shall wipe away all tears" from the eyes of those in paradise, we read in the book of many promises. And if the "Spirits of the dead" are enabled to return and see all that is going on on earth, and especially *in their homes,* what kind of bliss can be in store for them?

WHY THEOSOPHISTS DO NOT BELIEVE IN THE RETURN OF PURE "SPIRITS"

ENQ. What do you mean? Why should this interfere with their bliss?

THEO. Simply this; and here is an instance. A mother dies, leaving behind her little helpless children — orphans whom she adores — perhaps a beloved husband also. We say that her "Spirit" or *Ego* — that individuality which is now all impregnated, for the entire Devachanic period, with the noblest feelings held by its late *personality, i.e.,* love for her children, pity for those who suffer, and so on — we say that it is now entirely separated from the "vale of tears," that its future bliss consists in that blessed ignorance of all the woes it left behind. Spiritualists say, on the contrary, that it is as vividly aware of them, *and more so than before,* for "Spirits see more than mortals in the flesh do." We say that the bliss of the *Devachanee* consists in its complete conviction that it has never left the earth, and that there is no such thing as death at all; that the *post-mortem* spiritual *consciousness* of the mother will represent to her that she lives surrounded by her children and all those whom she loved; that no gap, no link, will be missing to make her disembodied state the most perfect and absolute happiness. The Spiritualists deny this point blank. According to their doctrine, unfortunate man is not liberated even by death from the sorrows of this life. Thus, the loving wife, who during her lifetime was ready to save her husband sorrow at the price of her heart's blood, is now doomed to see, in utter helplessness, his despair, and to register every hot tear he sheds for her loss. Is such a state of knowledge consistent with bliss? Then "bliss" stands in such a case for the greatest curse, and orthodox damnation must be a relief in comparison to it!

ENQ. But how does your theory avoid this? How can you reconcile the theory of Soul's omniscience with its blindness to that which is taking place on earth?

THEO. Because such is the law of love and mercy. During every Devachanic period the Ego, omniscient as it is *per se,* clothes itself, so to say, with the *reflection* of the personality that was. I have just told you that the *ideal* efflorescence of all the abstract, therefore undying and eternal qualities or attributes, such as love and mercy, the love of the good, the true and the beautiful, that ever spoke in the heart of the living personality, clung after death to the Ego, and therefore followed it to Devachan. For the time being, then, the Ego becomes the ideal reflection of the human being it was when last on earth, and *that* is not omniscient. Were it that, it would never be in the state we call Devachan at all.

ENQ. What are your reasons for it?

THEO. If you want an answer on the strict lines of our philosophy, then I will say that it is because everything is *illusion (Maya)* outside of eternal truth, which has neither form, colour, nor limitation. He who has placed himself beyond the veil of maya — and such are the highest Adepts and Initiates — can have no Devachan. As to the ordinary mortal, his bliss in it is complete. It is an *absolute* oblivion of all that gave it pain or sorrow in the past incarnation, and even oblivion of the fact that such things as pain or sorrow exist at all. The *Devachanee* lives its intermediate cycle between two incarnations surrounded by everything it had aspired to in vain, and in the companionship of everyone it loved on earth. It has reached the fulfilment of all its soul-yearnings. And thus it lives throughout long centuries an existence of *unalloyed* happiness, which is the reward for its sufferings in earth-life. In short, it bathes in a sea of uninterrupted felicity spanned only by events of still greater felicity in degree.

ENQ. But this is more than simple delusion, it is an existence of insane hallucinations!

THEO. From your standpoint it may be, not so from that of philosophy. Besides which, is not our whole terrestrial life filled with such delusions? Have you never met men and women living for years in a fool's paradise? I say it again, such oblivion and *hallucination* — if you call it so — are only a merciful law of nature and strict justice. To believe that a pure spirit can feel happy while doomed to witness the sins, mistakes, treachery, and, above all, the sufferings of those from whom it is severed by death and whom it loves best, without being able to help them, would be a maddening thought.

ENQ. There is something in your argument. I confess to having never seen it in this light.

THEO. Just so, and one must be selfish to the core and utterly devoid of the sense of retributive justice, to have ever imagined such a thing. We are with those whom we have lost in material form, and far, far nearer to them now, than when they were alive. And it is not only in the fancy of the *Devachanee,* as some may imagine, but in reality. For pure divine love is not merely the blossom of a human heart, but has its roots in eternity. Spiritual holy love is immortal, and Karma brings sooner or later all those who loved each other with such a spiritual affection to incarnate once more in the same family group. Again we say that love beyond the grave, illusion though you may call it, has a magic and divine potency which reacts on the living. A mother's *Ego* filled with love for the imaginary children it sees near itself, living a life of happiness, as real to *it* as when on earth — that love will always be felt by the children in flesh. It will manifest in their dreams, and often in various events — in *providential* protections and escapes, for love is a strong shield, and is not limited by space or time. As with this Devachanic "mother," so with the rest of human relationships and attachments, save the purely selfish or material. Analogy will suggest to you the rest.

ENQ. In no case, then, do you admit the possibility of the communication of the living with the *disembodied* spirit?

THEO. Yes, there is a case, and even two exceptions to the rule. The first exception is during the few days that follow immediately the death of a person and before the *Ego* passes into the Devachanic state. Whether any living mortal, save a few exceptional cases (when the intensity of the desire in the dying person to return for some purpose forced the higher consciousness *to remain awake,* and therefore it was really the *individuality,* the "Spirit" that communicated) has derived much benefit from the return of the spirit into the *objective* plane is another question. The spirit is dazed after death and falls very soon into what we call "*pre-devachanic* unconsciousness." The second exception is found in the *Nirmanakayas.*

ENQ. What about them? And what does the name mean for you?

THEO. It is the name given to those who, though they have won the right to Nirvana and cyclic rest — (*not* Devachan, as the latter is an illusion of our consciousness, a happy dream, and as those who are fit for Nirvana must have lost entirely every desire or possibility of the world's illusions) — have out of pity for mankind and those they left on earth renounced the Nirvanic state. Such an adept, or Saint, or whatever you may call him, believing it a selfish act to rest in bliss while mankind groans under the burden of misery produced by ignorance, renounces Nirvana, and determines to remain invisible *in spirit* on this earth. They have no material body, as they have left it behind; but otherwise they remain with all their principles even *in astral life* in our sphere. And such can and do communicate with a few elect ones, only surely not with *ordinary* mediums.

ENQ. I have put you the question about *Nirmanakayas* because I read in some German and other works that it was the name given to the terrestrial appearances or bodies assumed by Buddhas in the Northern Buddhistic teachings.

THEO. So they are, only the Orientalists have confused this terrestrial body by understanding it to be *objective* and *physical* instead of purely astral and subjective.

ENQ. And what good can they do on earth?

THEO. Not much, as regards individuals, as they have no right to interfere with Karma, and can only advise and inspire mortals for the general good. Yet they do more beneficent actions than you imagine.

ENQ. To this science would never subscribe, not even modern psychology. For them, no portion of intelligence can survive the physical brain. What would you answer them?

THEO. I would not even go to the trouble of answering, but would simply say, in the words given to "M. A. Oxon.," "Intelligence *is* perpetuated after the body is dead. Thought is not a question of the brain only. . . . It is reasonable to propound the indestructibility of the human spirit from what we know" (*Spirit Identity,* p. 69) .

ENQ. But "M. A. Oxon." is a Spiritualist?

THEO. Quite so, and the only *true* Spiritualist I know of, though we may still disagree with him on many a minor question. Apart from this, no Spiritualist comes nearer to the occult truths than he does. Like any one of us he speaks incessantly "of the surface dangers that beset the ill-equipped, feather-headed muddler with the occult, who crosses the threshold without counting the cost." I accept the three propositions he embodied in his address of July, 1884.

ENQ. What are these propositions?

THEO. 1. That there is a life coincident with, and independent of the physical life of the body.

    2. That, as a necessary corollary, this life extends beyond the life of the body (we say it extends throughout Devachan).

    3. That there is communication between the denizens of that state of existence and those of the world in which we now live.

All depends, you see, on the minor and secondary aspects of these fundamental propositions. Everything depends on the views we take of Spirit and Soul, or *Individuality* and *Personality*. Spiritualists confuse the two "into one"; we separate them, and say that, with the exceptions above enumerated, no *Spirit* will revisit the earth, though the animal Soul may. But let us return once more to our direct subject, the Skandhas.

ENQ. I begin to understand better now. It is the Spirit, so to say, of those Skandhas which are the most ennobling, which, attaching themselves to the incarnating Ego, survive, and are added to the stock of its angelic experiences. And it is the attributes connected with the material Skandhas, with selfish and personal motives, which, disappearing from the field of action between two incarnations, reappear at the subsequent incarnation as Karmic results to be atoned for; and therefore the Spirit will not leave Devachan. Is it so?

Theo. Very nearly so. If you add to this that the law of retribution, or Karma, rewarding the highest and most spiritual in Devachan, never fails to reward them again on earth by giving them a further development, and furnishing the Ego with a body fitted for it, then you will be quite correct.

A FEW WORDS ABOUT THE SKANDHAS

Enq. What becomes of the other, the lower Skandhas of the personality, after the death of the body? Are they quite destroyed?

Theo. They are and yet they are not — a fresh metaphysical and occult mystery for you. They are destroyed as the working stock in hand of the personality; they remain as *Karmic effects,* as germs, hanging in the atmosphere of the terrestrial plane, ready to come to life, as so many avenging fiends, to attach themselves to the new personality of the Ego when it reincarnates.

Enq. This really passes my comprehension, and is very difficult to understand.

Theo. Not once that you have assimilated all the details. For then you will see that for logic, consistency, profound philosophy, divine mercy and equity, this doctrine of Reincarnation has not its equal on earth. It is a belief in a perpetual progress for each incarnating Ego, or divine soul, in an evolution from the outward into the inward, from the material to the Spiritual, arriving at the end of each stage at absolute unity with the divine Principle. From strength to strength, from the beauty and perfection of one plane to the greater beauty and perfection of another, with accessions of new glory, of fresh knowledge and power in each cycle, such is the destiny of every Ego, which thus becomes its own Saviour in each world and incarnation.

Enq. But let us return, now that the subject of the Skandhas is disposed of, to the question of the consciousness which

survives death. Do we possess more knowledge in Devachan than we do in Earth life?

THEO. In one sense, we can acquire more knowledge; that
is, we can develop further any faculty which we loved
and strove after during life, provided it is concerned
with abstract and ideal things, such as music, painting,
poetry, etc., since Devachan is merely an idealized and
subjective continuation of earth-life.

ENQ. But if in Devachan the Spirit is free from matter, why
should it not possess all knowledge?

THEO. Because, as I told you, the Ego is, so to say, wedded
to the memory of its last incarnation. Thus, if you
think over what I have said, and string all the facts
together, you will realize that the Devachanic state is
not one of omniscience, but a transcendental continuation of the personal life just terminated. It is the rest
of the soul from the toils of life.

ENQ. But the scientific materialists assert that after the
death of man nothing remains; that the human body
simply disintegrates into its component elements; and
that what we call soul is merely a temporary self-consciousness produced as a by-product of organic action,
which will evaporate like steam. Is not theirs a strange
state of mind?

THEO. Not strange at all, that I see. If they say that self-
consciousness ceases with the body, then in their case
they simply utter an unconscious prophecy, for once
they are firmly convinced of what they assert, no conscious after-life is possible for them. For there *are* exceptions to every rule.

ON POST-MORTEM AND POST-NATAL CONSCIOUSNESS

ENQ. But if human self-consciousness survives death as a
rule, why should there be exceptions?

THEO. In the fundamental principles of the spiritual world no exception is possible. But there are rules for those who see, and rules for those who prefer to remain blind.

ENQ. Quite so, I understand. This is but an aberration of the blind man, who denies the existence of the sun because he does not see it. But after death his spiritual eyes will certainly compel him to see. Is that what you mean?

THEO. He will not be compelled, nor will he see anything. Having persistently denied during life the continuance of existence after death, he will be unable to see it, because his spiritual capacity having been stunted in life, it cannot develop after death, and he will remain blind. By insisting that he *must* see it, you evidently mean one thing and I another. You speak of the spirit from the spirit, or the flame from the flame — of Atma, in short — and you confuse it with the human soul — Manas. . . . You do not understand me; let me try to make it clear. The whole gist of your question is to know whether, in the case of a downright materialist, the complete loss of self-consciousness and self-perception after death is possible? Isn't it so? I answer, It is possible. Because, believing firmly in our Esoteric Doctrine, which refers to the *post-mortem* period, or the interval between two lives or births, as merely a transitory state, I say, whether that interval between two acts of the illusionary drama of life lasts one year or a million, that *post-mortem* state may, without any breach of the fundamental law, prove to be just the same state as that of a man who is in a dead faint.

ENQ. But since you have just said that the fundamental laws of the after death state admit of no exceptions, how can this be?

THEO. Nor do I say that it does admit of an exception. But the spiritual law of continuity applies only to things which are truly real. It is sufficient to understand what we mean by Buddhi and the duality of Manas to gain a clear perception why the materialist may fail to have a self-conscious survival after death. Since Manas, in its lower aspects, is the seat of the terrestrial mind, it can, therefore, give only that perception of the Universe which is based on the evidence of that mind; it cannot give spiritual vision. It is said in the Eastern school that between Buddhi and Manas (the *Ego*), or Iswara and Prajna* there is in reality no more difference than *between a forest and its trees, a lake and its waters.*

ENQ. But, as I understand it, Buddhi represents in this simile the forest, and Manas-taijasa† the trees. And if Buddhi is immortal, how can that which is similar to it, *i.e.,* Manas-taijasa, entirely lose its consciousness till the day of its new incarnation? I cannot understand it.

THEO. You cannot, because you will mix up an abstract representation of the whole with its casual changes of form. Remember that if it can be said of Buddhi-Manas that it is unconditionally immortal, the same cannot be said of the lower Manas, still less of Taijasa, which is merely an attribute. Neither of these, neither Manas nor Taijasa, can exist apart from Buddhi, the divine soul, because the first (*Manas*) is, in its lower aspect, a qualificative attribute of the terrestrial personality, and the second (*Taijasa*) is identical with the first, because it is the same Manas only with the light of Buddhi reflected on it. In its turn, Buddhi would remain only an impersonal spirit without this element which it borrows from the human soul, which conditions and makes of it, in this illusive Universe, *as it were something separate* from the universal soul for the whole period of the cycle of incarnation. Say rather that *Buddhi-Manas* can neither die nor lose its compound self-con-

---

* Iswara is the collective consciousness of the manifested deity, Brahma, *i.e.,* the collective consciousness of the Host of Dhyan Chohans (*vide* THE SECRET DOCTRINE); and Prajna is their individual wisdom.

† *Taijasa* means the radiant in consequence of its union with Buddhi; *i.e.,* Manas, the human soul, illuminated by the radiance of the divine soul. Therefore, Manas-taijasa may be described as radiant mind; the *human* reason lit by the light of the spirit; and Buddhi-Manas is the revelation of the divine *plus* human intellect and self-consciousness.

sciousness in Eternity, nor the recollection of its previous incarnations in which the two — *i.e.,* the spiritual
and the human soul — had been closely linked together.
But it is not so in the case of a materialist, whose human
soul not only receives nothing from the divine soul, but
even refuses to recognize its existence. You can hardly
apply this axiom to the attributes and qualifications of
the human soul, for it would be like saying that because
your divine soul is immortal, therefore the bloom on
your cheek must also be immortal; whereas this bloom,
like Taijasa, is simply a transitory phenomenon.

ENQ. Do I understand you to say that we must not mix in
our minds the noumenon with the phenomenon, the
cause with its effect?

THEO. I do say so, and repeat that, limited to Manas or the
human soul alone, the radiance of Taijasa itself becomes a mere question of time; because both immortality and consciousness after death become, for the terrestrial personality of man, simply conditioned attributes, as they depend entirely on conditions and beliefs
created by the human soul itself during the life of its
body. Karma acts incessantly: we reap *in our after-life*
only the fruit of that which we have ourselves sown in
this.

ENQ. But if my Ego can, after the destruction of my body,
become plunged in a state of entire unconsciousness,
then where can be the punishment for the sins of my
past life?

THEO. Our philosophy teaches that Karmic punishment
reaches the Ego only in its next incarnation. After death
it receives only the reward for the unmerited sufferings
endured during its past incarnation.* The whole pun-

---

* Some Theosophists have taken exception to this phrase, but the words are
those of Master, and the meaning attached to the word "unmerited"
is that given above. The essential idea was that men often suffer from
the effects of the actions done by others, effects which thus do not
strictly belong to their own Karma — and for these sufferings they of
course deserve compensation.

ishment after death, even for the materialist, consists, therefore, in the absence of any reward, and the utter loss of the consciousness of one's bliss and rest. Karma is the child of the terrestrial Ego, the fruit of the actions of the tree which is the objective personality visible to all, as much as the fruit of all the thoughts and even motives of the spiritual "I"; but Karma is also the tender mother, who heals the wounds inflicted by her during the preceding life, before she will begin to torture this Ego by inflicting upon him new ones. If it may be said that there is not a mental or physical suffering in the life of a mortal which is not the direct fruit and consequence of some sin in a preceding existence; on the other hand, since he does not preserve the slightest recollection of it in his actual life, and feels himself not deserving of such punishment, and therefore thinks he suffers for no guilt of his own, this alone is sufficient to entitle the human soul to the fullest consolation, rest, and bliss in his *post-mortem* existence. Death comes to our spiritual selves ever as a deliverer and friend. For the materialist, who, notwithstanding his materialism, was not a bad man, the interval between the two lives will be like the unbroken and placid sleep of a child, either entirely dreamless, or filled with pictures of which he will have no definite perception; while for the average mortal it will be a dream as vivid as life, and full of realistic bliss and visions.

ENQ. Then the personal man must always go on suffering *blindly* the Karmic penalties which the Ego has incurred?

THEO. Not quite so. At the solemn moment of death every man, even when death is sudden, sees the whole of his past life marshalled before him, in its minutest details. For one short instant the *personal* becomes one with the *individual* and all-knowing *Ego*. But this instant is enough to show to him the whole chain of causes which have been at work during his life. He sees and now understands himself as he is, unadorned by flattery or self-deception. He reads his life, remaining as a spectator looking down into the arena he is quitting; he feels and knows the justice of all the suffering that has overtaken him.

ENQ. Does this happen to everyone?

THEO. Without any exception. Very good and holy men see, we are taught, not only the life they are leaving, but even several preceding lives in which were produced the causes that made them what they were in the life just closing. They recognize the law of Karma in all its majesty and justice.

ENQ. Is there anything corresponding to this before rebirth?

THEO. There is. As the man at the moment of death has a retrospective insight into the life he has led, so, at the moment he is reborn on to earth, the *Ego,* awaking from the state of Devachan, has a prospective vision of the life which awaits him, and realizes all the causes that have led to it. He realizes them and sees futurity, because it is between Devachan and rebirth that the *Ego* regains his full *manasic* consciousness, and rebecomes for a short time the god he was, before, in compliance with Karmic law, he first descended into matter and incarnated in the first man of flesh. The "golden thread" sees all its "pearls" and misses not one of them.

WHAT IS REALLY MEANT BY ANNIHILATION

ENQ. I have heard some Theosophists speak of a golden thread on which their lives were strung. What do they mean by this?

THEO. In the Hindu Sacred books it is said that that which undergoes periodical incarnation is the *Sutratma,* which means literally the "Thread Soul." It is a synonym of the reincarnating Ego — Manas conjoined with *Buddhi* — which absorbs the Manasic recollections of all our preceding lives. It is so called, because, like the pearls on a thread, sǫ is the long series of human lives strung together on that one thread.

ENQ. Let us return to the materialist who, while not denying dreams, which he could hardly do, yet denies immortality in general and the survival of his own individuality.

THEO. And the materialist, without knowing it, is right. One who has no inner perception of, and faith in, the immortality of his soul, in that man the soul can never become Buddhi-taijasi, but will remain simply Manas, and for Manas alone there is no immortality possible. In order to live in the world to come a conscious life, one has to believe first of all in that life during the terrestrial existence. On these two aphorisms of the Secret Science all the philosophy about the *post-mortem* consciousness and the immortality of the soul is built. The Ego receives always according to its deserts. After the dissolution of the body, there commences for it a period of full awakened consciousness, or a state of chaotic dreams, or an utterly dreamless sleep undistinguishable from annihilation, and these are the three kinds of sleep. I repeat it: *death is sleep*. After death, before the spiritual eyes of the soul, begins a performance according to a programme learnt and very often unconsciously composed by ourselves: the practical carrying out of *correct* beliefs or of illusions which have been created by ourselves.

ENQ. The materialist, disbelieving in everything that cannot be proven to him by his five senses, or by scientific reasoning, based exclusively on the data furnished by these senses in spite of their inadequacy, and rejecting every spiritual manifestation, accepts life as the only conscious existence. Therefore according to their beliefs so will it be unto them. They will lose their personal Ego, and will plunge into a dreamless sleep until a new awakening. Is it so?

THEO. Almost so. Remember the practically universal teaching of the two kinds of conscious existence: the terrestrial and the spiritual. The latter must be considered real from the very fact that it is inhabited by the eternal, changeless and immortal Monad; whereas the incarnating Ego dresses itself up in new garments entirely different from those of its previous incarnations, and in which all except its spiritual prototype is doomed to a change so radical as to leave no trace behind.

ENQ. How so? Can my conscious terrestrial "I" perish not only for a time, like the consciousness of the materialist, but so entirely as to leave no trace behind?

THEO. According to the teaching, it must so perish and in its fulness, all except the principle which, having united itself with the Monad, has thereby become a purely spiritual and indestructible essence, one with it in the Eternity. But in the case of an out-and-out materialist, in whose personal "I" no Buddhi has ever reflected itself, how can the latter carry away into the Eternity one particle of that terrestrial personality? Your spiritual "I" is immortal; but from your present self it can carry away into Eternity that only which has become worthy of immortality, namely, the aroma alone of the flower that has been mown by death.

ENQ. Well, and the flower, the terrestrial "I"?

THEO. The flower, as all past and future flowers which have blossomed and will have to blossom on the mother bough, the *Sutratma,* all children of one root or Buddhi — will return to dust. Your present "I," as you yourself know, is not the body now sitting before me, nor yet is it what I would call Manas-Sutratma, but Sutratma-Buddhi.

ENQ. But this does not explain to me, at all, why you call life after death immortal, infinite and real, and the terrestrial life a simple phantom or illusion; since even that *post-mortem* life has limits, however much wider they may be than those of terrestrial life.

THEO. No doubt. The spiritual Ego of man moves in eternity
like a pendulum between the hours of birth and death.
But if these hours, marking the periods of life terrestrial
and life spiritual, are limited in their duration, and if
the very number of such stages in Eternity between
sleep and awakening, illusion and reality, has its beginning and its end, on the other hand, the spiritual pilgrim
is eternal. Therefore are the hours of his *post-mortem*
life, when, disembodied, he stands face to face with truth
and not the mirages of his transitory earthly existences,
during the period of that pilgrimage which we call "the
cycle of rebirths" — the only reality in our conception.
Such intervals, their limitation notwithstanding, do not
prevent the Ego, while ever perfecting itself, from following undeviatingly, though gradually and slowly, the
path to its last transformation, when that Ego, having
reached its goal, becomes a divine being. These intervals and stages help towards this final result instead
of hindering it; and without such limited intervals the
divine Ego could never reach its ultimate goal. I have
given you once already a familiar illustration by comparing the *Ego,* or the *individuality,* to an actor, and
its numerous and various incarnations to the parts it
plays. Will you call these parts or their costumes the
individuality of the actor himself? Like that actor, the
Ego is forced to play during the cycle of necessity, up
to the very threshold of *Paranirvana,* many parts such
as may be unpleasant to it. But as the bee collects its
honey from every flower, leaving the rest as food for
the earthly worms, so does our spiritual individuality,
whether we call it Sutratma or Ego. Collecting from
every terrestrial personality, into which Karma forces
it to incarnate, the nectar alone of the spiritual qualities
and self-consciousness, it unites all these into one whole
and emerges from its chrysalis as the glorified Dyhan
Chohan.

ENQ. Thus, then, it seems that, for the terrestrial personality,
immortality is still conditional. Is, then, immortality
itself *not* unconditional?

THEO. Not at all. But immortality cannot touch the *non-existent*: for all that which exists as SAT, or emanates from SAT, immortality and Eternity are absolute. Matter is the opposite pole of spirit, and yet the two are one. The essence of all this, *i.e.,* Spirit, Force and Matter, or the three in one, is as endless as it is beginningless; but the form acquired by this triple unity during its incarnations, its externality, is certainly only the illusion of our personal conceptions. Therefore do we call Nirvana and the Universal life alone a reality, while relegating the terrestrial life, its terrestrial personality included, and even its Devachanic existence, to the phantom realm of illusion.

DEFINITE WORDS FOR DEFINITE THINGS

ENQ. Don't you think it is because there are no definite and fixed terms to indicate each Principle in man, that a confusion of ideas arises in our minds with respect to the respective functions of these Principles?

THEO. The whole trouble has arisen from this: we have started our expositions of, and discussion about, the Principles, using their Sanskrit names instead of coining immediately, for the use of Theosophists, their equivalents in English. We must try and remedy this now.

ENQ. You will do well, as it may avoid further confusion; no two theosophical writers, it seems to me, have hitherto agreed to call the same Principle by the same name.

THEO. The confusion is more apparent than real, however. I have heard some of our Theosophists express surprise at, and criticize several essays speaking of these principles; but, when examined, there was no worse mistake in them than that of using the word "Soul" to cover the three principles without specifying the distinctions.

To avoid henceforth such misapprehensions, I propose to translate literally from the Occult Eastern terms their equivalents in English, and offer these for future use.

THE HIGHER
SELF is
{ Atma, the inseparable ray of the Universal and ONE SELF. It is the God *above*, more than within, us. Happy the man who succeeds in saturating his *inner Ego* with it!

THE SPIRITUAL
divine EGO, is
{ the Spiritual soul or *Buddhi*, in close union with *Manas*, the mind-principle, without which it is no Ego at all, but only the Atmic *Vehicle*.

THE INNER, or
HIGHER Ego is
{ *Manas*, the "Fifth" Principle, so called, independently of Buddhi. The Mind-Principle is only the Spiritual Ego when merged *into one* with Buddhi. It is the permanent *Individuality* or the "Reincarnating Ego."

THE LOWER,
or PERSONAL
Ego is
{ the physical man in conjunction with his *lower* Self, *i.e.*, animal instincts, passions, desires, etc. It is called the "false personality," and consists of the *lower Manas* combined with Kama-rupa, and operating through the Physical body and its phantom or "double."

The remaining Principle *"Prana,"* or "Life," is, strictly speaking, the radiating force or Energy of Atma — as the Universal Life and the ONE SELF — ITS lower or rather (in its effects) more physical, because manifesting, aspect. Prana or Life permeates the whole being of the objective Universe; and is called a "principle" only because it is an indispensable factor and the *deus ex machina* of the living man.

X

ON THE NATURE OF OUR THINKING
PRINCIPLE

THE MYSTERY OF THE EGO

ENQ. It is stated that the Skandhas — memory included —
change with every new incarnation. And yet, it is asserted that the reflection of the past lives, which, we are
told, are entirely made up of Skandhas, "must survive."
At the present moment I am not quite clear in my mind
as to what it is precisely that survives, and I would like
to have it explained. What is it? Is it only that "reflection," or those Skandhas, or always that same EGO, the
Manas?

THEO. I have just explained that the reincarnating Principle,
or that which we call the *divine* man, is indestructible
throughout the life cycle: indestructible as a thinking
Entity, and even as an ethereal form. The "reflection"
is only the spiritualized *remembrance,* during the Devachanic period, of the *ex-personality,* Mr. A. or Mrs.
B. — with which the *Ego* identifies itself during that
period. Since the latter is but the continuation of the
earth-life, so to say, the very acme and pitch, in an unbroken series, of the few happy moments in that now
past existence, the *Ego* has to identify itself with the
personal consciousness of that life, if anything shall
remain of it.

ENQ. This means that the *Ego,* notwithstanding its divine
nature, passes every such period between two incarnations in a state of mental obscuration, or temporary insanity.

THEO. Believing that, outside the ONE Reality, nothing is
better than a passing illusion — the whole Universe in-

cluded — we do not view it as insanity, but as a very
natural sequence or development of the terrestrial life.
What is life? A bundle of the most varied experiences,
of daily changing ideas, emotions, and opinions. In
our youth we are often enthusiastically devoted to an
ideal, to some hero or heroine whom we try to follow
and revive; a few years later, when the freshness of our
youthful feelings has faded out and sobered down, we
are the first to laugh at our fancies. And yet there was
a day when we had so thoroughly identified our own
personality with that of the ideal in our mind — especially if it was that of a living being — that the former was
entirely merged and lost in the latter. Can it be said
of a man of fifty that he is the same being that he was
at twenty? The *inner* man is the same; the outward living personality is completely transformed and changed.
Would you also call these changes in the human mental
states insanity?

ENQ. How would *you* name them, and especially how would
you explain the permanence of one and the evanescence
of the other?

THEO. The clue lies in the double consciousness of our mind,
and also, in the dual nature of the mental "principle."
There is a spiritual consciousness, the Manasic mind
illumined by the light of Buddhi, that which subjective-
ly perceives abstractions; and the sentient consciousness (the lower *Manasic* light), inseparable from our
physical brain and senses. This latter consciousness is
held in subjection by the brain and physical senses, and,
being in its turn equally dependent on them, must of
course fade out and finally die with the disappearance
of the brain and physical senses. It is only the former
kind of consciousness, whose root lies in eternity, which
survives and lives for ever, and may, therefore, be regarded as immortal. Everything else belongs to passing
illusions.

ENQ. How is it that MANAS, although you call it *Nous,* a
"God," is so weak during its incarnations, as to be

actually conquered and fettered by its body?

THEO. I might retort with the same question and ask: "How is it that he, whom you regard as 'the God of Gods' and the One living God, *is so weak* as to allow evil (or the Devil) to have the best of *him* as much as of all his creatures, whether while he remains in Heaven or during the time he was incarnated on this earth?" You are sure to reply again: "This is a Mystery; and we are forbidden to pry into the mysteries of God." Not being forbidden to do so by our religious philosophy, I answer your question that, unless a God descends as an *Avatara,* no divine principle can be otherwise than cramped and paralysed by turbulent, animal matter. Heterogeneity will always have the upper hand over homogeneity, on this plane of illusions, and the nearer an essence is to its root-principle, Primordial Homogeneity, the more difficult it is for the latter to assert itself on earth. Spiritual and divine powers lie dormant in every human Being; and the wider the sweep of his spiritual vision the mightier will be the God within him. But as few men can feel that God, and since, as an average rule, deity is always bound and limited in our thought by earlier conceptions, those ideas that are inculcated in us from childhood, therefore, it is difficult for you to understand our philosophy.

ENQ. And is it this Ego of ours which is our God?

THEO. Not at all; *"A* God" is not the universal deity, but only a spark from the one ocean of Divine Fire. Our God *within* us, or "our Father in Secret" is what we call the "HIGHER SELF," *Atma.* Our incarnating Ego was a God in its origin, as were all the primeval emanations of the One Unknown Principle. But since its "fall into Matter," having to incarnate throughout the cycle, in succession, from first to last, it is no longer a free and happy god, but a poor pilgrim on his way to regain that which he has lost. I can answer you more fully by repeating what is said of the INNER MAN in ISIS UNVEILED (Vol. II, 593) :

From the remotest antiquity *mankind* as a whole *have always been convinced of the existence of a personal spiritual entity within the personal physical man.* This inner entity was more or less divine, according to its proximity to the *crown* — Christos. The closer the union the more serene man's destiny, the less dangerous the external conditions. This belief is neither bigotry nor superstition, only an ever-present, instinctive feeling of the proximity of another spiritual and invisible world, which, though it be subjective to the senses of the outward man, is perfectly objective to the inner ego. Furthermore, they believed that *there are external and internal conditions which affect the determination of our will upon our actions.* They rejected fatalism, for fatalism implies a blind course of some still blinder power. But they believed in *destiny* [or *Karma*], which from birth to death every man is weaving thread by thread around himself, as a spider does his cobweb; and this destiny is guided either by that presence termed by some the guardian angel, or our more intimate astral inner man, who is but too often the evil genius of the man of flesh [or the *personality*]. Both these lead on the outward man, but one of them must prevail; and from the very beginning of the invisible affray the stern and implacable *law of compensation* [*and retribution*] steps in and takes its course, following faithfully the fluctuating [of the conflict]. When the last strand is woven, and man is seemingly enwrapped in the network of his own doing then he finds himself completely under the empire of this *self-made* destiny. It then either fixes him like the inert shell against the immovable rock, or like a feather carries him away in a whirlwind raised by his own actions.

Such is the destiny of the MAN — the true Ego, not the Automaton, the *shell* that goes by that name. It is for him to become the conqueror over matter.

THE COMPLEX NATURE OF MANAS

ENQ. But you wanted to tell me something of the essential nature of Manas, and of the relation in which the Skandhas of physical man stand to it?

THEO. It is this nature, mysterious, Protean, beyond any grasp, and almost shadowy in its correlations with the other principles, that is most difficult to realize, and still more so to explain. Manas is a principle, and yet it is an Entity and individuality or Ego. He is a "God," and yet he is doomed to an endless cycle of incarnations, for each of which he is made responsible, and for each of which he has to suffer. If I would make myself comprehensible, I must begin at the beginning and give you the genealogy of this Ego in a few lines.

ENQ. Say on.

THEO. Try to imagine a "Spirit," a celestial Being, whether we call it by one name or another, divine in its essential nature, yet not pure enough to be *one with the* ALL, and having, in order to achieve this, to so purify its nature as to finally gain that goal. It can do so only by passing *individually* and *personally, i.e.,* spiritually and physically, through every experience and feeling that exists in the manifold or differentiated Universe. It has, therefore, after having gained such experience in the lower kingdoms, and having ascended higher and still higher with every rung on the ladder of being, to pass through every experience on the human planes. In its very essence it is THOUGHT, and is, therefore, called in its plurality *Manasa-putras,* "the Sons of the (Universal) mind." This *individualized* "Thought" is what we Theosophists call the *real* human Ego, the thinking Entity imprisoned in a case of flesh and bones. This is surely a Spiritual Entity, not *Matter,* and such Entities are the incarnating Egos that inform the bundle of animal matter called mankind, and whose names are *Manasa* or "Minds." But once imprisoned, or incarnate, their essence becomes dual: that is to say, the *rays* of the eternal divine Mind, considered as individual entities, assume a twofold attribute which is (*a*) their *essential* inherent characteristic, heaven-aspiring mind (higher *Manas*), and (*b*) the human quality of thinking, or animal cogitation, rationalized owing to the superiority of the human brain, the *Kama*-tending or lower Manas. One gravitates towards Buddhi, the other, tending downwards, to the seat of passions and animal desires. The latter have no room in Devachan, nor can they associate with the divine triad which ascends as ONE into mental bliss. Yet it is the Ego, the Manasic Entity, which is held responsible for all the sins of the lower attributes, just as a parent is answerable for the transgressions of his child, so long as the latter remains irresponsible.

ENQ. Is this "child" the personality?

THEO. It is. When, therefore, it is stated that the personality dies with the body it does not state all. The body, which was only the objective symbol of Mr. A. or Mrs. B., fades away with all its material Skandhas, which are the visible expressions thereof. But all that which constituted during life the *spiritual* bundle of experiences, the noblest aspirations, undying affections, and *unselfish* nature of Mr. A. or Mrs. B., clings for the time of the Devachanic period to the EGO, which is identified with the spiritual portion of that terrestrial Entity, now passed away out of sight. The ACTOR is so imbued with the *role* just played by him that he dreams of it during the whole Devachanic night, which *vision* continues till the hour strikes for him to return to the stage of life to enact another part.

THE DOCTRINE IS TAUGHT IN ST. JOHN'S GOSPEL

ENQ. Does Christ teach anything of the sort?

THEO. He does; and every well-informed Occultist and even Kabalist will tell you so. Christ, or the fourth Gospel at any rate, teaches reincarnation as also the annihilation of the personality, if you but forget the dead letter and hold to the esoteric Spirit. Remember verses 1 to 6 in ch. xv of *St. John*. What does the parable speak about if not of the *upper triad* in man? *Atma* is the Husbandman, the Spiritual Ego or *Buddhi* (Christos) the Vine, while the animal and vital Soul, the *personality,* is the "branch." "I am the *true* vine, and my Father is the Husbandman. Every branch in me that beareth not fruit he taketh away . . . As the branch cannot bear fruit of itself except it abide in the vine; no more can ye, except ye abide in me. I am the Vine, ye are the branches. . . . If a man abide not in me, he is cast forth as a branch, and is *withered;* and men gather them and cast them into the fire and they are burned."

Now we explain it in this way. We say that the Husbandman means Atma, the Symbol for the infinite, impersonal Principle,* while the Vine stands for the Spiritual Soul, *Christos,* and each branch represents a new incarnation.

ENQ. But what proofs have you to support such an arbitrary interpretation?

THEO. Universal symbology is a warrant for its correctness and that it is not arbitrary. Hermas† says of "God" that he "planted the Vineyard," *i.e.,* he created mankind. In the *Kabala,* it is shown that the Aged of the Aged, or the "Long Face," plants a vineyard, the latter typifying mankind; and a vine, meaning Life. The Spirit of *"King* Messiah" is, therefore, shown as washing his garments in *the wine* from above, from the creation of the world.‡ And King *Messiah* is the EGO purified *by washing his garments* (*i.e.,* his personalities in rebirth), in the *wine from* above, or BUDDHI. Adam, or A-Dam, is "blood." The Life of the flesh is in the blood (nephesh — soul), *Leviticus,* xvii, II. And Adam-Kadmon is the Only-Begotten. Noah also plants a vineyard — the allegorical hot-bed of future humanity. As a consequence of the adoption of the same allegory, we find it reproduced in the Nazarene *Codex.* Seven vines are

---

* During the *Mysteries,* it is the Hierophant, the "Father," who planted the Vine. Every symbol has Seven Keys to it. The discloser of the *Pleroma* was always called "Father."

† [*Hermas Pastor,* similitude v, § 6.]

‡ *Zohar,* Comm. on *Genesis,* xl, 10.

procreated — which seven vines are our Seven Races with their seven Saviours or *Buddhas* — which spring from Kebar-Zivo, and Ferho (or Parcha) Raba waters them.* When the blessed will ascend among the creatures of Light, they shall see Iavar-Zivo, *Lord of* LIFE, and the First VINE.† These kabalistic metaphors are thus naturally repeated in the *Gospel according to St. John* (xv, I).

Let us not forget that in the human system — even according to those philosophies which ignore our septenary division — the EGO or *thinking man* is called the *Logos,* or the Son of Soul and Spirit. "Manas is the adopted Son of King —— and Queen ——" (esoteric equivalents for Atma and Buddhi), says an occult work. He is the "man-god" of Plato, who crucifies himself in *Space* (or the duration of the life cycle) for the redemption of MATTER. This he does by incarnating over and over again, thus leading mankind onward to perfection, and making thereby room for lower forms to develop into higher. Not for one life does he cease progressing himself and helping all physical nature to progress; even the occasional, very rare event of his losing one of his personalities, in the case of the latter being entirely devoid of even a spark of spirituality, helps toward his individual progress.

ENQ. But surely, if the *Ego* is held responsible for the transgressions of its personalities, it has to answer also for the loss, or rather the complete annihilation, of one of such.

THEO. Not at all, unless it has done nothing to avert this dire fate. But if, all its efforts notwithstanding, its voice, *that of our conscience,* was unable to penetrate through the wall of matter, then the obtuseness of the latter, proceeding from the imperfect nature of the material, is classed with other failures of nature. The Ego is sufficiently punished by the loss of Devachan, and especially by having to incarnate almost immediately.

---

* *Codex Nazaraeus,* Vol. III, pp. 60, 61.
† *Ibid.,* Vol. II, p. 281.

ENQ. This doctrine of the possibility of losing one's soul — or personality, do you call it? — militates against the ideal theories of both Christians and Spiritualists, though Swedenborg adopts it to a certain extent, in what he calls *Spiritual death*. They will never accept it.

THEO. This can in no way alter a fact in nature, if it be a fact, or prevent such a thing occasionally taking place. The universe and everything in it, moral, mental, physical, psychic, or Spiritual, is built on a perfect law of equilibrium and harmony. As said before (*vide Isis Unveiled,* I, 318-19), the centripetal force could not manifest itself without the centrifugal in the harmonious revolutions of the spheres; and all forms and their progress are the products of this dual force in nature. Now the Spirit (or *Buddhi*) is the centrifugal and the soul (*Manas*) the centripetal spiritual energy; and to produce one result they have to be in perfect union and harmony. Break or damage the centripetal motion of the earthly soul tending toward the centre which attracts it; arrest its progress by clogging it with a heavier weight of matter than it can bear, or than is fit for the Devachanic state, and the harmony of the whole will be destroyed. Personal life, or perhaps rather its ideal reflection, can only be continued if sustained by the twofold force, that is by the close union of *Buddhi* and *Manas* in every rebirth or personal life. The least deviation from harmony damages it; and when it is destroyed beyond redemption the two forces separate at the moment of death. During a brief interval the *personal* form (called indifferently *Kama-rupa* and *Mayavi-rupa*), the spiritual efflorescence of which, attaching itself to the Ego, follows it into Devachan and gives to the permanent *individuality* its *personal* colouring (*pro tem.*, so to speak), is carried off to remain in *Kama-loka* and to be gradually annihilated. For it is after the death of the utterly depraved, the unspiritual and the wicked beyond redemption, that arrives the critical and supreme moment. If during life the ultimate and desperate effort of the INNER SELF (*Manas*), to unite something of the personality with itself and the high glimmering ray of the divine Buddhi, is thwarted; if this ray is allowed to be more and more shut out from the ever-thickening crust of physical brain, the Spiritual EGO or Manas, once freed from the body, remains severed entirely from the ethereal relic of the personality; and the latter, or *Kama-rupa*, following its earthly attractions, is drawn into and remains in *Hades*, which we call the *Kama-loka*. Annihilation, however, is never instantaneous, and may require centuries sometimes for its accomplishment. But there the personality remains along with the *remnants* of other more fortunate personal Egos, and becomes with them a *shell* and an *Elementary*.

ENQ. But does not the author of *Isis Unveiled* stand accused of having preached against reincarnation?

THEO. By those who have misunderstood what was said, yes. At the time that work was written, reincarnation was not believed in by any Spiritualists, either English or American, and what is said there of *reincarnation* was directed against the French Spiritists, whose theory is as unphilosophical and absurd as the Eastern teaching is logical and self-evident in its truth. How can the author of *Isis* argue against *Karmic* reincarnation, at long intervals varying between 1,000 and 1,500 years, when it is the fundamental belief of both Buddhists and Hindus?

ENQ. Then you reject the theories of both the Spiritists and the Spiritualists, in their entirety?

THEO. Not in their entirety, but only with regard to their respective fundamental beliefs. We believe with the Spiritualists and the Spiritists in the existence of "Spirits," or invisible Beings endowed with more or less intelligence. But, while in our teachings their kinds and *genera* are legion, our opponents admit of no other than human disembodied "Spirits," which, to our knowledge, are mostly Kama-lokic SHELLS.

ENQ. Don't you believe in their phenomena at all?

THEO. It is because I believe in them with too good reason, and (save some cases of deliberate fraud) know them to be as true as that you and I live, that all my being revolts against them. Once more I speak only of physical, not mental or even psychic phenomena. Like attracts like. There are several high-minded, pure, good men and women, known to me personally, who have passed years of their lives under the direct guidance and even protection of high "Spirits," whether disembodied or planetary. These Intelligences guide and control mortals only in rare and exceptional cases to which they are attracted and magnetically drawn by the Karmic past of the individual. It is not enough to sit "for development" in order to attract them. That only opens the door to a swarm of "spooks," good, bad and indifferent, to which the medium becomes a slave for life. It is against such promiscuous mediumship and intercourse with goblins that I raise my voice, not against spiritual mysticism. The latter is ennobling and holy; the former is of just the same nature as the phenomena of two centuries ago, for which so many witches and wizards have been made to suffer.

ENQ. Do you mean to suggest that it is all witchcraft and nothing more?

THEO. What I mean is that, whether conscious or unconscious, all this dealing with the dead is *necromancy,* and a most dangerous practice. For ages before Moses such raising of the dead was regarded by all the intelligent nations as sinful and cruel, inasmuch as it disturbs the rest of the souls and interferes with their evolutionary development into higher states. The collective wisdom of all past centuries has ever been loud in denouncing such practices. Finally, I say: While some of the so-called "spirits" do not know what they are talking about, repeating merely — like poll-parrots — what they find in the medium's and other people's brains, others are most dangerous, and can only lead one to evil.

XI

ON THE MYSTERIES OF REINCARNATION

PERIODICAL REBIRTHS

ENQ. You mean, then, that we have all lived on earth before, in many past incarnations, and shall go on so living?

THEO. I do. The life-cycle, or rather the cycle of conscious life, begins with the separation of the mortal animal-man into sexes, and will end with the close of the last generation of men, in the seventh round and seventh race of mankind. Considering we are only in the fourth round and fifth race, its duration is more easily imagined than expressed.

ENQ. And we keep on incarnating in new *personalities* all the time?

THEO. Most assuredly so; because this life-cycle or period of incarnation may be best compared to human life. As each such life is composed of days of activity separated by nights of sleep or of inaction, so, in the incarnation-cycle, an active life is followed by a Devachanic rest.

ENQ. And it is this succession of births that is generally defined as reincarnation?

THEO. Just so. It is only through these births that the perpetual progress of the countless millions of Egos toward final perfection and final rest (as long as was the period of activity) can be achieved.

ENQ. And what is it that regulates the duration, or special qualities of these incarnations?

THEO. Karma, the universal law of retributive justice.

ENQ. Is it an intelligent law?

THEO. For us, no adjective or qualification could describe that which is impersonal and no entity, but a universal operative law. If you question me about the causative intelligence in it, I must answer you I do not know. But if you ask me to define its effects and tell you what these are in our belief, I may say that the experience of thousands of ages has shown us that they are absolute and unerring *equity, wisdom,* and *intelligence.* For Karma in its effects is an unfailing redresser of human injustice, and of all the failures of nature; a stern adjuster of wrongs; a retributive law which rewards and punishes with equal impartiality. It is, in the strictest sense, "no respecter of persons," though, on the other hand, it can neither be propitiated, nor turned aside by prayer.

ENQ. Are we then to infer a man's past from his present?

THEO. Only so far as to believe that his present life is what it justly should be, to atone for the sins of the past life. Of course — seers and great adepts excepted — we cannot as average mortals know what those sins were. From our paucity of data, it is impossible for us even to determine what an old man's youth must have been; neither can we, for like reasons, draw final conclusions merely from what we see in the life of some man, as to what his past life may have been.

WHAT IS KARMA?

ENQ. But what is Karma?

THEO. As I have said, we consider it as the *Ultimate Law* of the Universe, the source, origin and fount of all other laws which exist throughout Nature. Karma is the unerring law which adjusts effect to cause, on the physical, mental and spiritual planes of being. As no cause remains without its due effect from greatest to least, from a cosmic disturbance down to the movement of your hand, and as like produces like, *Karma* is that unseen and unknown law *which adjusts wisely, intelligently and equitably* each effect to its cause, tracing the latter back to its producer. Though itself *unknowable,* its action is perceivable.

ENQ. Then it is the "Absolute," the "Unknowable" again, and is not of much value as an explanation of the problems of life?

THEO. On the contrary. For, though we do not know what Karma is *per se,* and in its essence, we *do* know *how* it works, and we can define and describe its mode of action with accuracy. We only do *not* know its ultimate *Cause,* just as modern philosophy universally admits that the *ultimate* Cause of anything is "unknowable."

ENQ. And what has Theosophy to say in regard to the solution of the more practical needs of humanity?

THEO. To be pointed, according to our teaching all these great social evils, the distinction of classes in Society, and of the sexes in the affairs of life, the unequal distribution of capital and of labour — all are due to what we tersely but truly denominate KARMA.

ENQ. But, surely, all these evils which seem to fall upon the masses somewhat indiscriminately are not actual merited and INDIVIDUAL Karma?

THEO. No, they cannot be so strictly defined in their effects as to show that each individual environment, and the particular conditions of life in which each person finds himself, are nothing more than the retributive Karma which the individual generated in a previous life. We must not lose sight of the fact that every atom is subject to the general law governing the whole body to which it belongs, and here we come upon the wider track of the Karmic law. Do you not perceive that the aggregate of individual Karma becomes that of the nation to which those individuals belong, and further, that the sum total of National Karma is that of the World? The evils that you speak of are not peculiar to the individual or even to the Nation, they are more or less universal; and it is upon this broad line of Human interdependence that the law of Karma finds its legitimate and equable issue.

ENQ. Do I, then, understand that the law of Karma is not necessarily an individual law?

THEO. That is just what I mean. It is impossible that Karma could readjust the balance of power in the world's life and progress unless it had a broad and general line of action. It is held as a truth among Theosophists that the interdependence of Humanity is the cause of what is called Distributive Karma, and it is this law which affords the solution to the great question of collective suffering and its relief. It is an occult law, moreover, that no man can rise superior to his individual failings, without lifting, be it ever so little, the whole body of which he is an integral part. In the same way, no one can sin, nor suffer the effects of sin, alone. In reality, there is no such thing as "Separateness"; and the nearest approach to that selfish state, which the laws of life permit, is in the intent or motive.

ENQ. And are there no means by which the distributive or national Karma might be concentrated or collected, so to speak, and brought to its natural and legitimate fulfilment without all this protracted suffering?

THEO. As a general rule, and within certain limits which define the age to which we belong, the law of Karma cannot be hastened or retarded in its fulfilment. But of this I am certain, the point of possibility in either of these directions has never yet been touched.

ENQ. But alas! there seems no immediate hope of any relief short of an earthquake, or some such general ingulfment!

THEO. What right have we to think so while one-half of humanity is in a position to effect an immediate relief of the privations which are suffered by their fellows?

When every individual has contributed to the general good what he can of money, of labour, and of ennobling thought, then, and only then, will the balance of National Karma be struck. It is reserved for heroic souls to find out the cause of this unequal pressure of retributive Karma, and by a supreme effort to readjust the balance of power, and save the people from a moral ingulfment a thousand times more disastrous and more permanently evil than the like physical catastrophe, in which you seem to see the only possible outlet for this accumulated misery.

ENQ. Well, then, tell me generally how you describe this law of Karma?

THEO. We describe Karma as that Law of readjustment which ever tends to restore disturbed equilibrium in the physical, and broken harmony in the moral world. We say that Karma does not act in this or that particular way always; but that it always *does* act so as to restore Harmony and preserve the balance of equilibrium, in virtue of which the Universe exists.

ENQ. Give me an illustration.

THEO. Think now of a pond. A stone falls into the water and creates disturbing waves. These waves oscillate backwards and forwards till at last, owing to the operation of what physicists call the law of the dissipation of energy, they are brought to rest, and the water returns to its condition of calm tranquillity. Similarly *all* action, on every plane, produces disturbance in the balanced harmony of the Universe, and the vibrations so produced will continue to roll backwards and forwards, if its area is limited, till equilibrium is restored. But since each such disturbance starts from some particular point, it is clear that equilibrium and harmony can only be restored by the reconverging *to that same point* of all the forces which were set in motion from it.

ENQ. But I see nothing of a moral character about this law. It looks to me like the simple physical law that action and reaction are equal and opposite.

THEO. We say that "Good" and "Harmony," and "Evil" and "Disharmony," are synonymous. Further we maintain that all pain and suffering are results of want of Harmony, and that the one terrible and only cause of the disturbance of Harmony is *selfishness* in some form or another. Hence Karma gives back to every man the *actual consequences* of his own actions, without any regard to their moral character; but since he receives his due for *all*, it is obvious that he will be made to atone for all sufferings which he has caused, just as he will reap in joy and gladness the fruits of all the happiness and harmony he had helped to produce.

ENQ. I wish you could give some concrete example of the action of Karma?

THEO. That I cannot do. We can only feel sure, as I said before, that our present lives and circumstances are the direct results of our own deeds and thoughts in lives that are past. But we, who are not Seers or Initiates, cannot know anything about the details of the working of the law of Karma.

ENQ. Can anyone, even an Adept or Seer, follow out this Karmic process of readjustment in detail?

THEO. Certainly: "Those who *know*" can do so by the exercise of powers which are latent even in all men.

WHO ARE THOSE WHO KNOW?

ENQ. Does this hold equally of ourselves as of others?

THEO. Equally. As just said, the same limited vision exists for all, save those who have reached in the present incarnation the acme of spiritual vision and clairvoyance. We can only perceive that, if things with us ought to have been different, they would have been different; that we are what we have made ourselves, and have only what we have earned for ourselves.

ENQ. I am afraid such a conception would only embitter us.

THEO. I believe it is precisely the reverse. It is disbelief in
    the just law of retribution that is more likely to awaken
    every combative feeling in man. A child, as much as a
    man, resents a punishment, or even a reproof he believes
    to be unmerited, far more than he does a severer punish-
    ment, if he feels that it is merited. Belief in Karma is
    the highest reason for reconcilement to one's lot in this
    life, and the very strongest incentive towards effort to
    better the succeeding rebirth. Both of these, indeed,
    would be destroyed if we supposed that our lot was the
    result of anything but strict *Law,* or that destiny was
    in any other hands than our own.

ENQ. You have just asserted that this system of Reincarnation
    under Karmic law commended itself to reason, justice,
    and the moral sense. But, if so, is it not at some sacrifice
    of the gentler qualities of sympathy and pity, and thus
    a hardening of the finer instincts of human nature?

THEO. Only apparently, not really. No man can receive
    more or less than his deserts without a corresponding
    injustice or partiality to others; and a law which could
    be averted through compassion would bring about more
    misery than it saved, more irritation and curses than
    thanks. Remember also, that we do not administer the
    law, if we do create causes for its effects; it administers
    itself; and again, that the most copious provision for the
    manifestation of *just* compassion and mercy is shown in
    the state of Devachan.

ENQ. You speak of Adepts as being an exception to the rule
    of our general ignorance. Do they really know more
    than we do of Reincarnation and after states?

THEO. They do, indeed. By the training of faculties we all
    possess, but which they alone have developed to perfec-
    tion, they have entered in spirit these various planes and
    states we have been discussing. For long ages, one gen-
    eration of Adepts after another has studied the my-
    steries of being, of life, death, and rebirth, and all have

taught in their turn some of the facts so learned.

ENQ. And is the production of Adepts the aim of Theosophy?

THEO. Theosophy considers humanity as an emanation from divinity on its return path thereto. At an advanced point upon the path, Adeptship is reached by those who have devoted several incarnations to its achievement. For, remember well, no man has ever reached Adeptship in the Secret Sciences in one life; but many incarnations are necessary for it after the formation of a conscious purpose and the beginning of the needful training. Many may be the men and women in the very midst of our Society who have begun this uphill work toward illumination several incarnations ago, and who yet, owing to the personal illusions of the present life, are either ignorant of the fact, or on the road to losing every chance in this existence of progressing any farther. They feel an irresistible attraction toward occultism and the *Higher Life,* and yet are too personal and self-opinionated, too much in love with the deceptive allurements of mundane life and the world's ephemeral pleasures, to give them up; and so lose their chance in their present birth. But, for ordinary men, for the practical duties of daily life, such a far-off result is inappropriate as an aim and quite ineffective as a motive.

ENQ. What, then, may be their object or distinct purpose in joining the Theosophical Society?

THEO. Many are interested in our doctrines and feel instinctively that they are truer than those of any dogmatic religion. Others have formed a fixed resolve to attain the highest ideal of man's duty.

THE DIFFERENCE BETWEEN FAITH AND KNOWLEDGE; OR, BLIND AND REASONED FAITH

ENQ. You say that they accept and believe in the doctrines of Theosophy. But, as they do not belong to those Adepts you have just mentioned, then they must accept your teachings on *blind faith*. In what does this differ from that of conventional religions?

THEO. What you call "faith," and that which is *blind faith,* in reality, and with regard to the dogmas of the Christian religions, becomes with us *"knowledge,"* the logical sequence of things *we know,* about *facts* in nature. Your Doctrines are based upon interpretation, therefore, upon the *second-hand* testimony of Seers; ours upon the invariable and unvarying testimony of Seers. The ordinary Christian theology, for instance, holds that man is a creature of God, of three component parts — body, soul, and spirit — all essential to his integrity, and all, either in the gross form of physical earthly existence or in the etherealized form of post-resurrection experience, needed to so constitute him for ever, each man having thus a permanent existence separate from other men, and from the Divine. Theosophy, on the other hand, holds that man, being an emanation from the Unknown, yet ever present and infinite Divine Essence, his body and everything else is impermanent, hence an illusion; Spirit alone in him being the one enduring substance, and even that losing its separated individuality at the moment of its complete reunion with the *Universal Spirit.*

ENQ. If we lose even individuality, then it becomes simply annihilation.

THEO. I say it *does not,* since I speak of *separate,* not of universal individuality. The latter becomes as a part transformed into the whole; the *dewdrop* is not evaporated, but becomes the sea. Is physical man *annihilated,* when from a foetus he becomes an old man?

ENQ. It follows, then, that there is, *de facto,* no man, but all is Spirit?

THEO. You are mistaken. It thus follows that the union of Spirit with matter is but temporary; or, to put it more clearly, since Spirit and matter are one, being the two opposite poles of the *universal* manifested substance —

that Spirit loses its right to the name so long as the smallest particle and atom of its manifesting substance still clings to any form, the result of differentiation. To believe otherwise is *blind faith.*

ENQ. Thus it is on *knowledge,* not on *faith,* that you assert that the permanent principle, the Spirit, simply makes a transit through matter?

THEO. I would put it otherwise and say — we assert that the appearance of the permanent and *one* principle, Spirit, *as matter* is transient, and, therefore, no better than an illusion.

ENQ. Very well; and this, given out on knowledge not faith?

THEO. Just so. But as I see very well what you are driving at, I may just as well tell you that we hold *faith,* such as you advocate, to be a mental disease, and real faith, *i.e.,* the *pistis* of the Greeks, as *"belief based on knowledge,"* whether supplied by the evidence of physical or *spiritual* senses.

ENQ. What do you mean?

THEO. I mean, if it is the difference between the two that you want to know, then I can tell you that between *faith on authority* and *faith on one's spiritual intuition* there is a very great difference.

ENQ. What is it?

THEO. One is human credulity and *superstition,* the other human belief and *intuition.*

ENQ. And is it that "intuition" which forces you to reject God as a personal Father, Ruler and Governor of the Universe?

THEO. Precisely. We believe in an ever unknowable Principle, because blind aberration alone can make one maintain that the Universe, thinking man, and all the marvels contained even in the world of matter, could have grown without some *intelligent powers* to bring about the extraordinary wise arrangement of all its parts. Nature may err, and often does, in its details and the external manifestations of its materials, never in its inner causes and results.

ENQ. Faith for faith, is not the faith of the Christian who believes, in his human helplessness and humility, that there is a merciful Father in Heaven who will protect him from temptation, help him in life, and forgive him his transgressions, better than the cold and proud, almost fatalistic faith of the Buddhists, Vedantins, and Theosophists?

THEO. Persist in calling our belief "faith" if you will. But once we are again on this ever-recurring question, I ask in my turn: faith for faith, is not the one based on strict logic and reason better than the one which is based simply on human authority or — hero-worship? Yours is a faith, moreover, which clashes not only with every conceivable view of justice and logic, but which, if analysed, leads man to his moral perdition, checks the progress of mankind, and positively making of might, right — transforms every second man into a Cain to his brother Abel.

ENQ. What do you allude to?

HAS GOD THE RIGHT TO FORGIVE?

THEO. To the Doctrine of Atonement; I allude to that dangerous dogma which teaches us that no matter how enormous our crimes against the laws of God and of man, we have but to believe in the self-sacrifice of Jesus for the salvation of mankind, and his blood will wash out every stain. It is twenty years that I preach against it, and I may now draw your attention to a paragraph from *Isis Unveiled* [Vol. II, p. 542], written in 1877.

"God's mercy is boundless and unfathomable. It is impossible to conceive of a human sin so damnable that the price paid in advance for the redemption of the sinner would not wipe it out if a thousandfold worse. And furthermore, it is never too late to repent. Though the offender wait until the last minute of the last hour of the last day of his mortal life, before his blanched lips utter the confession of faith, he may go to Paradise; the dying thief did it, and so may all others as vile. These are the assumptions of the Church, and of the Clergy; assumptions banged at the heads of your countrymen by England's favourite preachers, right in the 'light of the XIXth century,' " this most paradoxical age of all. Now to what does it lead?

ENQ. Does it not make the Christian happier than the Buddhist or Brahmin?

THEO. No; not the educated man, at any rate, since the majority of these have long since virtually lost all belief in this cruel dogma. But it leads those who still believe in it more *easily to the threshold of every conceivable crime* than any other I know of. Let me quote to you from *Isis* once more (*vide* Vol. II, pp. 542-543) :

If we step outside the little circle of creed and consider the universe as a whole balanced by the exquisite adjustment of parts, how all sound logic, how the faintest glimmering sense of Justice revolts against this Vicarious Atonement! If the criminal sinned only against himself, and wronged no one but himself; if by sincere repentance he could cause the obliteration of past events, not only from the memory of man, but also from that imperishable record, which no deity — not even the Supremest of the Supreme — can cause to disappear, then this dogma might not be incomprehensible. But to maintain that one may wrong his fellow man, kill, disturb the equilibrium of society and the natural order of things, and then — through cowardice, hope, or compulsion, matters not — be forgiven by believing that the spilling of one blood washes out the other blood spilt — this is preposterous! Can the *results* of a crime be obliterated even though the crime itself should be pardoned? The effects of a cause are never limited to the boundaries of the cause, nor can the results of crime be confined to the offender and his victim. Every good as well as evil

action has its effects, as palpably as the stone flung into a
calm water. The simile is trite, but it is the best ever conceived, so let us use it. The eddying circles are greater and
swifter, as the disturbing object is greater or smaller, but
the smallest pebble, nay, the tiniest speck, makes its ripples.
And this disturbance is not alone visible and on the surface.
Below, unseen, in every direction — outward and downward
— drop pushes drop until the sides and bottom are touched
by the force. More, the air above the water is agitated,
and this disturbance passes, as the physicists tell us, from
stratum to stratum out into space forever and ever; an
impulse has been given to matter, and that is never lost,
can never be recalled! . . .

So with crime, and so with its opposite. The action may
be instantaneous, the effects are eternal. When, after the
stone is once flung into the pond, we can recall it to the
hand, roll back the ripples, obliterate the force expended,
restore the etheric waves to their previous state of non-
being, and wipe out every trace of the act of throwing the
missile, so that Time's record shall not show that it ever
happened, then, *then* we may patiently hear Christians
argue for the efficacy of this Atonement.

and — cease to believe in Karmic Law. As it now stands,
we call upon the whole world to decide which of our
two doctrines is the most appreciative of deific justice,
and which is more reasonable, even on simple human
evidence and logic.

ENQ. The ultimate destiny of man, then, is not a Heaven
presided over by God, but the gradual transformation
of matter into its primordial element, Spirit?

THEO. It is to that final goal to which all tends in nature.

ENQ. Do not some of you regard this association of "fall of
spirit into matter" as evil, and rebirth as a sorrow?

THEO. Some do, and therefore strive to shorten their period
of probation on earth. It is not an unmixed evil, however, since it ensures the experience upon which we
mount to knowledge and wisdom. I mean that experi-

ence which *teaches* that the needs of our spiritual nature can never be met by other than spiritual happiness. As long as we are in the body, we are subjected to pain, suffering and all the disappointing incidents occurring during life. Therefore, and to palliate this, we finally acquire knowledge which alone can afford us relief and and hope of a better future.

XII

WHAT IS PRACTICAL THEOSOPHY?

DUTY

ENQ. Why, then, the need for rebirths, since all alike fail to secure a permanent peace?

THEO. Because the final goal cannot be reached in any way but through life experiences, and because the bulk of these consist in pain and suffering. It is only through the latter that we can learn. Joys and pleasures teach us nothing; they are evanescent, and can only bring in the long run satiety. Moreover, our constant failure to find any permanent satisfaction in life which would meet the wants of our higher nature shows us plainly that those wants can be met only on their own plane, to wit — the spiritual.

ENQ. Is the natural result of this a desire to quit life by one means or another?

THEO. If you mean by such desire "suicide," then I say, most decidedly not. Such a result can never be a "natural" one, but is ever due to a morbid brain disease, or to most decided and strong materialistic views. It is the worst of crimes and dire in its results. But if by desire, you mean simply aspiration to reach spiritual existence, not a wish to quit the earth, then I would call it a very natural desire indeed. Otherwise voluntary death would be an abandonment of our present post and of the duties incumbent on us, as well as an attempt to shirk Karmic responsibilities, and thus involve the creation of new Karma.

ENQ. But if actions on the material plane are unsatisfying,

why should duties, which are such actions, be impera-
tive?

THEO. First of all, because our philosophy teaches us that
the object of doing our duties to all men, and to ourselves the last, is not the attainment of personal happiness, but of the happiness of others; the fulfilment of
right for the sake of right, not for what it may bring
us. Happiness, or rather contentment, may indeed follow the performance of duty, but is not and must not
be the motive for it.

ENQ. And how would you define these duties, or "duty," in
general, as you understand the term?

THEO. Duty is that which *is due* to Humanity, to our fellow
men, neighbours, family, and especially that which we
owe to all those who are poorer and more helpless than
we are ourselves. This is a debt which, if left unpaid
during life, leaves us spiritually insolvent and moral
bankrupts in our next incarnation. Theosophy is the
quintessence of *duty.* Finally: if you ask me how we
understand Theosophical duty practically and in view
of Karma, I may answer you that our duty is to drink
without a murmur to the last drop whatever contents
the cup of life may have in store for us, to pluck the
roses of life only for the fragrance they may shed on
others, and to be ourselves content but with the thorns,
if that fragrance cannot be enjoyed without depriving
some one else of it.

ENQ. What do you consider as due to humanity at large?

THEO. Full recognition of equal rights and privileges for
all, and without distinction of race, colour, social position, or birth.

ENQ. When would you consider such due not given?

THEO. When there is the slightest invasion of another's
right — be that other a man or a nation; when there
is any failure to show him the same justice, kindness,
consideration or mercy which we desire for ourselves.

The whole present system of politics is built on the oblivion of such rights, and the most fierce assertion of national selfishness.

ENQ. Do you take any part in politics?

THEO. As a Society, we carefully avoid them, for the reasons given below. To seek to achieve political reforms before we have effected a reform in *human nature, is like putting new wine into old bottles.* Make men feel and recognize in their innermost hearts what is their real, true duty to all men, and every old abuse of power, every iniquitous law in the national policy, based on human, social or political selfishness, will disappear of itself. Foolish is the gardener who seeks to weed his flower bed of poisonous plants by cutting them off from the surface of the soil, instead of tearing them out by the roots. No lasting political reform can be ever achieved with the same selfish men at the head of affairs as of old.

THE RELATIONS OF THE T. S. TO POLITICAL REFORMS

ENQ. The Theosophical Society is not, then, a political organization?

THEO. Certainly not. It is international in the highest sense in that its members comprise men and women of all races, creeds, and forms of thought, who work together for one object, the improvement of humanity; but as a society it takes absolutely no part in any national or party politics.

ENQ. Why is this?

THEO. Just for the reasons I have mentioned. Moreover, political action must necessarily vary with the circumstances of the time and with the idiosyncrasies of individuals. While from the very nature of their position as Theosophists the members of the T. S. are agreed on the principles of Theosophy, or they would not belong to the society at all, it does not thereby follow that they agree on every other subject. As a society they can only act together in matters which are common to all — that is, in Theosophy itself; as individuals, each is left perfectly free to follow out his or her particular line of political thought and action, so long as this does not conflict with Theosophical principles or hurt the Theosophical Society.

ENQ. But surely the T.S. does not stand altogether aloof from the social questions which are now so fast coming to the front?

THEO. The very principles of the T.S. are a proof that it does not — or, rather, that most of its members do not — so stand aloof. If humanity can only be developed mentally and spiritually by the enforcement, first of all, of the soundest and most scientific physiological laws, it is the bounden duty of all who strive for this development to do their utmost to see that those laws shall be generally carried out. All Theosophists are only too sadly aware that, in Occidental countries especially, the social condition of large masses of the people renders it impossible for either their bodies or their spirits to be properly trained, so that the development of both is thereby arrested. As this training and development is one of the express objects of Theosophy, the T. S. is in thorough sympathy and harmony with all true efforts in this direction.

ENQ. But what do you mean by "true efforts"? Each social reformer has his own panacea, and each believes his to be the one and only thing which can improve and save humanity?

THEO. Perfectly true, and this is the real reason why so little satisfactory social work is accomplished. In most of these panaceas there is no really guiding principle, and there is certainly no one principle which connects them all. Valuable time and energy are thus wasted; for men, instead of cooperating, strive one against the other, often, it is to be feared, for the sake of fame and reward rather than for the great cause which they profess to have at heart, and which should be supreme in their lives.

ENQ. How, then, should Theosophical principles be applied so that social cooperation may be promoted and true efforts for social amelioration be carried on?

THEO. Let me briefly remind you what these principles are — universal Unity and Causation; Human Solidarity; the Law of Karma; Reincarnation. These are the four links of the golden chain which should bind humanity into one family, one Universal Brotherhood.

ENQ. How?

THEO. In the present state of society, especially in so-called civilized countries, we are continually brought face to face with the fact that large numbers of people are suffering from misery, poverty and disease. Their physical condition is wretched, and their mental and spiritual faculties are often almost dormant. On the other hand, many persons at the opposite end of the social scale are leading lives of careless indifference, material luxury, and selfish indulgence. Neither of these forms of existence is mere chance. Both are the effects of the conditions which surround those who are subject to them, and the neglect of social duty on the one side is most closely connected with the stunted and arrested development on the other. In sociology, as in all branches of true science, the law of universal causation holds good. But this causation necessarily implies, as its logical outcome, that human solidarity on which Theosophy so strongly insists. If the action of one reacts on the lives of all, and this is the true scientific idea, then it is only by all men becoming brothers and all women sisters, and by all practising in their daily lives true brotherhood and true sisterhood, that the real human solidarity, which lies at the root of the elevation of the race, can ever be attained. It is this action and interaction, this true brotherhood and sisterhood, in which each shall live for all and all for each, which is one of the fundamental Theosophical principles that every Theosophist should be bound, not only to teach, but to carry out in his or her individual life.

ENQ. All this is very well as a general principle, but how would you apply it in a concrete way?

THEO. Look for a moment at what you would call the concrete facts of human society. Contrast the lives not only of the masses of the people, but of many of those who are called the middle and upper classes, with what they might be under healthier and nobler conditions, where justice, kindness, and love were paramount, instead of the selfishness, indifference, and brutality which now too often seem to reign supreme. All good and evil things in humanity have their roots in human character, and this character is, and has been, conditioned by the endless chain of cause and effect. But this conditioning applies to the future as well as to the present and the past. Selfishness, indifference, and brutality can never be the normal state of the race — to believe so would be to despair of humanity — and that no Theosophist can do. Progress can be attained, and only attained, by the development of the nobler qualities. Now, true evolution teaches us that by altering the surroundings of the organism we can alter and improve the organism; and in the strictest sense this is true with regard to man. Every Theosophist, therefore, is bound to do his utmost to help on, by all the means in his power, every wise and well-considered social effort which has for its object the amelioration of the condition of the poor. Such efforts should be made with a view to their ultimate social emancipation, or the development of the sense of duty in those who now so often neglect it in nearly every relation of life.

ENQ. Agreed. But who is to decide whether social efforts are wise or unwise?

THEO. No one person and no society can lay down a hard and fast rule in this respect. Much must necessarily be left to the individual judgement. One general test may, however, be given. Will the proposed action tend to promote that true brotherhood which it is the aim of Theosophy to bring about? No real Theosophist will have much difficulty in applying such a test; once he is satisfied of this, his duty will lie in the direction of forming public opinion. And this can be attained only by inculcating those higher and nobler conceptions of public and private duties which lie at the root of all spiritual and material improvement. In every conceivable case he himself must be a centre of spiritual action, and from him and his own daily individual life must radiate those higher spiritual forces which alone can regenerate his fellow men.

ENQ. But why should he do this? Are not he and all, as you teach, conditioned by their Karma, and must not Karma necessarily work itself out on certain lines?

THEO. It is this very law of Karma which gives strength to all that I have said. The individual cannot separate himself from the race, nor the race from the individual. The law of Karma applies equally to all, although all are not equally developed. In helping on the development of others, the Theosophist believes that he is not only helping them to fulfil their Karma, but that he is also, in the strictest sense, fulfilling his own. It is the development of humanity, of which both he and they are integral parts, that he has always in view, and he knows that any failure on his part to respond to the highest within him retards not only himself but all, in their progressive march. By his actions, he can make it either more difficult or more easy for humanity to attain the next higher plane of being.

ENQ. How does this bear on the fourth of the principles you mentioned, *viz.*, Reincarnation?

THEO. The connection is most intimate. If our present lives

depend upon the development of certain principles which are a growth from the germs left by a previous existence, the law holds good as regards the future. Once grasp the idea that universal causation is not merely present, but past, present and future, and every action on our present plane falls naturally and easily into its true place, and is seen in its true relation to ourselves and to others. Every mean and selfish action sends us backward and not forward, while every noble thought and every unselfish deed are stepping-stones to the higher and more glorious planes of being. If this life were all, then in many respects it would indeed be poor and mean; but regarded as a preparation for the next sphere of existence, it may be used as the golden gate through which we may pass, not selfishly and alone, but in company with our fellows, to the palaces which lie beyond.

ON SELF-SACRIFICE

ENQ. Is equal justice to all and love to every creature the highest standard of Theosophy?

THEO. No; there is an even far higher one.

ENQ. What can it be?

THEO. The giving to others *more* than to oneself — *self-sacrifice*. Such was the standard and abounding measure which marked so pre-eminently the greatest Teachers and Masters of Humanity — *e.g.*, Gautama Buddha in history, and Jesus of Nazareth as in the Gospels. This trait alone was enough to secure to them the perpetual reverence and gratitude of the generations of men that come after them. We say, however, that self-sacrifice has to be performed with discrimination; and such a self-abandonment, if made without justice, or blindly, regardless of subsequent results, may often prove not only made in vain, but harmful. One of the fundamental rules of Theosophy is justice to oneself — viewed as a unit of collective humanity, not as a personal self-justice, not more but not less than to others; unless, indeed, by the sacrifice of the *one* self we can benefit the many.

ENQ. Could you make your idea clearer by giving an instance?

THEO. Self-sacrifice for practical good to save many, or several people, Theosophy holds as far higher than self-abnegation for a sectarian idea, such as that of "saving the heathen from *damnation*," for instance. In our opinion, Father Damien, the young man of thirty who offered his whole life in sacrifice for the benefit and alleviation of the sufferings of the lepers at Molokai, and who went to live for eighteen years alone with them, to finally catch the loathsome disease and die, *has not died in vain.* He has given relief and relative happiness to thousands of miserable wretches. He has brought to them consolation, mental and physical. He threw a streak of light into the black and dreary night of an existence, the hopelessness of which is unparalleled in the records of human suffering. He was a *true Theosophist,* and his memory will live for ever in our annals.

ENQ. Then you regard self-sacrifice as a duty?

THEO. We do; and explain it by showing that altruism is an integral part of self-development. But we have to discriminate. A man has no right to starve himself *to death* that another man may have food, unless the life of that man is obviously more useful to the many than is his own life. But it is his duty to sacrifice his own comfort, and to work for others if they are unable to work for themselves. It is his duty to give all that which is wholly his own and can benefit no one but himself if he selfishly keeps it from others. Theosophy teaches self-abnegation, but does not teach rash and useless self-sacrifice, nor does it justify fanaticism.

ENQ. But how are we to reach such an elevated status?

THEO. By the enlightened application of our precepts to practice. By the use of our higher reason, spiritual intuition and moral sense, and by following the dictates of what we call "the still small voice" of our conscience, which is that of our EGO, and which speaks louder in us than the earthquakes and the thunders of Jehovah, wherein "the Lord is not."

ENQ. If such are our duties to humanity at large, what do you understand by our duties to our immediate surroundings?

THEO. Just the same, *plus* those that arise from special obligations with regard to family ties.

ENQ. Then it is not true, as it is said, that no sooner does a man enter into the Theosophical Society than he begins to be gradually severed from his wife, children, and family duties?

THEO. It is a groundless calumny, like so many others. The first of the Theosophical duties is to do one's duty by *all* men, and especially by those to whom one's *specific* responsibilities are due, because one has either voluntarily undertaken them, such as marriage ties, or because one's destiny has allied one to them; I mean those we owe to parents or next of kin.

ENQ. And what may be the duty of a Theosophist to himself?

THEO. To control and conquer, *through the Higher, the lower self*. To purify himself inwardly and morally; to fear no one, and nought, save the tribunal of his own conscience. Never to do a thing by halves; *i.e.*, if he thinks it the right thing to do, let him do it openly and boldly, and if wrong, never touch it at all. It is the duty of a Theosophist to lighten his burden by thinking of the wise aphorism of Epictetus, who says: "Be not diverted from your duty *by any idle reflection the silly world may make upon you*, for their censures are not in your power, and consequently should not be any part of your concern."

ENQ. But suppose a member of your Society should plead inability to practise altruism by other people, on the ground that "charity begins at home"; urging that he is too busy, or too poor, to benefit mankind or even any of its units — what are your rules in such a case?

THEO. No man has a right to say that he can do nothing for others, on any pretext whatever. "By doing the proper duty in the proper place, a man may make the world his debtor," says an English writer. A cup of cold water given in time to a thirsty wayfarer is a nobler duty and more worth than a dozen of dinners given away, out of season, to men who can afford to pay for them. No man who has not got it in him will ever become a *Theosophist;* but he may remain a member of our Society all the same. We have no rules by which we could force any man to become a practical Theosophist, if he does not desire to be one.

ENQ. Then why does he enter the Society at all?

THEO. That is best known to him who does so. For, here again, we have no right to prejudge a person, not even if the voice of a whole community should be against him.

ON CHARITY

ENQ. How do you Theosophists regard the Christian duty of charity?

THEO. What charity do you mean? Charity of mind, or practical charity in the physical plane?

ENQ. I mean practical charity, as your idea of Universal brotherhood would include, of course, charity of mind.

THEO. Act individually and not collectively; follow the Northern Buddhist precepts: "Never put food into the mouth of the hungry by the hand of another"; "Never let the shadow of thy neighbor (*a third person*) come between thyself and the object of thy bounty"; "Never give to the Sun time to dry a tear before thou hast wiped it." Again "Never give money to the needy, or food to the priest, who begs at thy door, *through thy servants,* lest thy money should diminish gratitude, and thy food turn to gall."

ENQ. But how could this be applied practically?

THEO. The Theosophical ideas of charity mean *personal* exertion for others; *personal* mercy and kindness; *personal* interest in the welfare of those who suffer; *personal* sympathy, fore-thought and assistance in their troubles or needs. We believe in relieving the starvation of the soul, as much if not more than the emptiness of the stomach.

HOW MEMBERS CAN HELP THE SOCIETY

ENQ. How do you expect the Fellows of your Society to help in the work?

THEO. First by studying and comprehending the Theosophical doctrines, so that they may teach others, especially the young people. Secondly, by taking every opportunity of talking to others and explaining to them what Theosophy is, and what it is not; by removing misconceptions and spreading an interest in the subject. Thirdly, by assisting in circulating our literature, by buying books when they have the means, by lending and giving them and by inducing their friends to do so. Fourthly, by defending the Society from the unjust aspersions cast upon it, by every legitimate device in their power. Fifthly, and most important of all, by the example of their own lives.

ENQ. But all this literature, to the spread of which you attach so much importance, does not seem to me of much practical use in helping mankind. This is not practical charity.

THEO. We think otherwise. We hold that a good book which gives people food for thought, which strengthens and clears their minds, and enables them to grasp truths which they have dimly felt but could not formulate — we hold that such a book does a real, substantial good. As to what you call practical deeds of charity, to benefit the bodies of our fellow men, we do what little we can. What the Theosophist has to do above all is to forget his personality.

WHAT A THEOSOPHIST OUGHT NOT TO DO

ENQ. Have you any prohibitory laws or clauses for Theosophists in your Society?

THEO. Many, but, none of them are enforced. They express the ideal of our organization — but the practical application of such things we leave to the discretion of the Fellows themselves. This is precisely why I feel forced to lay such a stress on the difference between true Theosophy and its hard-struggling and well-intentioned, but still unworthy vehicle, the Theosophical Society.

ENQ. May I be told what are these perilous reefs in the open sea of Theosophy?

THEO. Well may you call them reefs, as more than one otherwise sincere and well-meaning F.T.S. has had his Theosophical canoe shattered into splinters on them! And yet to avoid certain things seems the easiest thing in the world to do. For instance, here is a series of such negatives, screening positive Theosophical duties:

No Theosophist should be silent when he hears evil reports or slanders spread about the Society, or innocent persons, whether they be his colleagues or outsiders.

ENQ. But suppose what one hears is the truth, or may be true without one knowing it?

THEO. Then you must demand good proofs of the assertion, and hear both sides impartially before you permit the

accusation to go uncontradicted. You have no right to
believe in evil, until you get undeniable proof of the
correctness of the statement.

ENQ. And what should you do then?

THEO. Pity and forbearance, charity and long-suffering,
ought to be always there to prompt us to excuse our sin-
ning brethren, and to pass the gentlest sentence possible
upon those who err. A Theosophist ought never to
forget what is due to the shortcomings and infirmities
of human nature.

ENQ. Ought he to forgive entirely in such cases?

THEO. In every case, especially he who is sinned against.

ENQ. But if by so doing, he risks to injure, or allow others
to be injured? What ought he to do then?

THEO. His duty; that which his conscience and higher nature suggests to him; but only after mature delibera-
tion. Justice consists in doing no injury to any living
being; but justice commands us also never to allow injury to be done to the many, or even to one innocent
person, by allowing the guilty one to go unchecked.

ENQ. What are the other negative clauses?

THEO. No Theosophist ought to be contented with an idle
or frivolous life, doing no real good to himself and still
less to others. He should work for the benefit of the
few who need his help if he is unable to toil for Humanity, and thus work for the advancement of the Theosophical cause.

ENQ. This demands an exceptional nature, and would come
rather hard upon some persons.

THEO. Then they had better remain outside the T. S. instead of sailing under false colours. No one is asked to
give more than he can afford, whether in devotion, time,
work or money.

ENQ. What comes next?

THEO. No working member should set too great value on his personal progress or proficiency in Theosophic studies; but must be prepared rather to do as much altruistic work as lies in his power. He should not leave the whole of the heavy burden and responsibility of the Theosophical movement on the shoulders of the few devoted workers. Each member ought to feel it his duty to take what share he can in the common work, and help it by every means in his power.

ENQ. This is but just. What comes next?

THEO. No Theosophist should place his personal vanity, or feelings, above those of his Society as a body. He who sacrifices the latter, or other people's reputations on the altar of his personal vanity, worldly benefit, or pride, ought not to be allowed to remain a member. One cancerous limb diseases the whole body.

ENQ. Is it the duty of every member to teach others and preach Theosophy?

THEO. It is indeed. No fellow has a right to remain idle, on the excuse that he knows too little to teach. For he may always be sure that he will find others who know still less than himself. And also it is not until a man begins to try to teach others that he discovers his own ignorance and tries to remove it. But this is a minor clause.

ENQ. What do you consider, then, to be the chief of these negative Theosophical duties?

THEO. To be ever prepared to recognize and confess one's faults. To rather sin through exaggerated praise than through too little appreciation of one's neighbour's efforts. Never to backbite or slander another person. Always to say openly and direct to his face anything you have against him. Never to make yourself the echo of anything you may hear against another, nor harbour revenge against those who happen to injure you.

ENQ. Where is the line of demarcation between backbiting and just criticism to be drawn? Is it not one's duty to warn one's friends and neighbors against those whom one knows to be dangerous associates?

THEO. If by allowing them to go on unchecked other persons may be thereby injured, it is certainly our duty to obviate the danger by warning them privately. But true or false, no accusation against another person should ever be spread abroad. If true, and the fault hurts no one but the sinner, then leave him to his Karma. If false, then you will have avoided adding to the injustice in the world. Therefore, keep silent about such things with every one not directly concerned. But if your discretion and silence are likely to hurt or endanger others, then I add: *Speak the truth at all costs,* and say, with Annesly, "Consult duty, not events." There are cases when one is forced to exclaim, "Perish discretion, rather than allow it to interfere with duty."

ENQ. Admitting yourself that there is at least as much, if not more, backbiting, slandering, and quarrelling in the T. S. as in the Christian Churches, let alone scientific societies — What kind of Brotherhood is this? I may ask.

THEO. A very poor specimen, indeed, as at present, and, until carefully sifted and reorganized, *no* better than all others. Remember, however, that human nature is the same *in* the Theosophical Society as *out* of it. Its members are no saints: they are at best sinners trying to do better, and liable to fall back owing to personal weakness.

ENQ. Your position does not seem to me a very enviable one.

THEO. It is not. But don't you think that there must be something very noble, very exalted, very true, behind the Society and its philosophy, when the leaders of the movement still continue to work for it with all their strength?

ENQ. I confess, such a perseverance seems to me very astounding, and I wondered why you did all this.

THEO. Believe me for no self-gratification. The coming generation will find the path to peace a little less thorny, and the way a little widened, and thus all this suffering will have produced good results, and their self-sacrifice will not have been in vain. At present, the main, fundamental object of the Society is to sow germs in the hearts of men, which may in time sprout, and under more propitious circumstances lead to a healthy reform, conducive of more happiness *to the masses* than they have hitherto enjoyed.

XIII

ON THE MISCONCEPTIONS ABOUT THE THEOSOPHICAL SOCIETY

THEOSOPHY AND ASCETICISM

ENQ. I have heard people say that your rules require all members to be vegetarians, celibates, and rigid ascetics; but you have not told me anything of the sort yet. Can you tell me the truth once for all about this?

THEO. The truth is that our rules require nothing of the kind. The Theosophical Society does not even expect, far less require, of *any* of its members that they should be ascetics in any way, except — if you call *that* asceticism — that they should try and benefit other people and be unselfish in their own lives.

ENQ. But still many of your members are strict vegetarians. This is most often the case with those who take a prominent part in connection with the work of your Society.

THEO. That is only natural. But I see that I had better give you an explanation of our views on the subject of asceticism in general, and then you will understand about vegetarianism and so on.

ENQ. Please proceed.

THEO. As I have already told you, most people who become really earnest students of Theosophy, and active workers in our Society, wish to do more than study theoretically the truths we teach. They wish to *know* the truth by their own direct personal experience, and to study Occultism, with the object of acquiring the wisdom and power which they feel that they need in order to help others effectually and judiciously, instead of blindly and at haphazard. The first thing which the members learn is a true conception of the relation of the body, or physical sheath, to the inner, the true man. The relation and mutual interaction between these two aspects of human nature are explained, so that they soon become imbued with the supreme importance of the inner man over the outer case or body.

ENQ. I see, you regard only *moral* asceticism as necessary. It is as a means to an end, that end being the perfect equilibrium of the *inner* nature of man, and the attainment of complete mastery over the body with all its passions and desires?

THEO. Just so. But these means must be used intelligently and wisely, not blindly and foolishly; like an athlete who is training and preparing for a great contest, not like the miser who starves himself into illness that he may gratify his passion for gold.

ENQ. I understand now your general idea; but let us see how you apply it in practice. How about vegetarianism, for instance?

THEO. One of the great German scientists has shown that every kind of animal tissue, however you may cook it, still retains certain marked characteristics of the animal which it belonged to, which characteristics can be recognized. And apart from that, everyone knows by the taste what meat he is eating. We go a step farther, and prove that when the flesh of animals is assimilated by man as food, it imparts to him, physiologically, some of the characteristics of the animal it came from. Moreover, occult science teaches and proves this to its students by ocular demonstration, showing also that this "coarsening" or "animalizing" effect on man is greatest from the flesh of the larger animals, less for birds, still less for fish and other cold-blooded animals, and least of all when he eats only vegetables.

ENQ. Then he had better not eat at all?

THEO. If he could live without eating, of course it would. But as the matter stands, he must eat to live, and so we advise really earnest students to eat such food as will least clog and weight their brains and bodies, and will have the smallest effect in hampering and retarding the development of their intuition, their inner faculties and powers.

ENQ. Then you do not adopt all the arguments which vegetarians in general are in the habit of using?

THEO. Certainly not. Some of their arguments are very weak, and often based on assumptions which are quite false. But, on the other hand, many of the things they say are quite true. For instance, we believe that much disease, and especially the great predisposition to disease which is becoming so marked a feature in our time, is very largely due to the eating of meat. But it would take too long to go thoroughly into this question of vegetarianism on its merits; so please pass on to something else.

ENQ. One question more. What are your members to do with regard to their food when they are ill?

THEO. Follow the best practical advice they can get, of course. Don't you grasp yet that we never impose any hard and fast obligations in this respect? Remember once for all that in all such questions we take a rational, and never a fanatical, view of things. If from illness or long habit a man cannot go without meat, why, by all means let him eat it. It is no crime; it will only retard his progress a little; for after all is said and done, the purely bodily actions and functions are of far less importance than what a man *thinks* and *feels,* what desires he encourages in his mind, and allows to take root and grow there.

ENQ. Then with regard to the use of wine and spirits, I suppose you do not advise people to drink them?

THEO. They are worse for his moral and spiritual growth

than meat, for alcohol in all its forms has a direct, marked, and very deleterious influence on man's psychic condition. Drinking is only less destructive to the development of the inner powers than the habitual use of hashish, opium, and similar drugs.

THEOSOPHY AND MARRIAGE

ENQ. Now to another question; must a man marry or remain a celibate?

THEO. It depends on the kind of man you mean. If you refer to one who intends to live *in* the world, one who, even though a good, earnest Theosophist, and an ardent worker for our cause, still has ties and wishes which bind him to the world; who, in short, does not feel that he has done for ever with what men call life, and that he desires one thing and one thing only — to know the truth, and to be able to help others — then for such a one I say there is no reason why he should not marry, if he likes to take the risks of that lottery where there are so many more blanks than prizes. Surely you cannot believe us so absurd and fanatical as to preach against marriage altogether? On the contrary, save in a few exceptional cases of practical Occultism, marriage is the only remedy against immorality.

ENQ. But why cannot one acquire this knowledge and power when living a married life?

THEO. My dear sir, I cannot go into physiological questions with you; but I can give you an obvious and, I think, a sufficient answer, which will explain to you the moral reasons we give for it. Can a man serve two masters? No! Then it is equally impossible for him to divide his attention between the pursuit of Occultism and a wife. If he tries to, he will assuredly fail in doing either properly; and, let me remind you, practical Occultism is far too serious and dangerous a study for a man to take up, unless he is in the most deadly earnest, and ready to sacrifice *all, himself first of all,* to gain his end. I am referring to those who are determined to tread that path of discipleship which leads to the highest goal.

WHY, THEN, IS THERE SO MUCH PREJUDICE AGAINST THE T.S.?

ENQ. If Theosophy is even half of what you say, why should there exist such ill-feeling against it?

THEO. It is; but you must bear in mind how many powerful adversaries we have aroused ever since the formation of our Society. As I just said, if the Theosophical movement were one of those numerous modern crazes, as harmless at the end as they are evanescent, it would be simply laughed at — as it is now by those who still do not understand its real purport — and left severely alone. But it is nothing of the kind. Intrinsically, Theosophy is the most serious movement of this age; and one, moreover, which threatens the very life of most of the time-honoured humbugs, prejudices, and social evils of the day.

ENQ. Cannot you give me more details so that I may know what to answer when asked — a brief history of the Society, in short; and why the world believes all this?

THEO. Most outsiders knew absolutely nothing of the Society itself, its motives, objects or beliefs. From its very beginning the world has seen in Theosophy nothing but certain marvellous phenomena. Very soon the Society came to be regarded as a body pretending to the possession of "miraculous" powers. The world never realized that the Society taught absolute disbelief in *miracle* or even the possibility of such; that in the Society there were only a few people who possessed such psychic powers and but few who cared for them. Nor did it understand that the phenomena were never produced publicly, but only privately for friends, and merely given as an accessory, to prove by direct demonstration that such things could be produced without dark rooms, spirits, mediums, or any of the usual paraphernalia. Unfortunately, this misconception was greatly strengthened and exaggerated by the first book on the subject which excited much attention in Europe — Mr. Sinnett's *The Occult World.*

ENQ. For what, and since when, do the Spiritualists hate you?

THEO. From the first day of the Society's existence. No sooner the fact became known that, as a body, the T. S. did not believe in communications with the spirits of the dead, but regarded the so-called "spirits" as, for the most part, astral reflections of disembodied personalities, shells, etc., than the Spiritualists conceived a violent hatred to us and especially to the Founders. This began in 1875 and continues to the present day. In 1879, the headquarters of the T. S. were transferred from New York to Bombay, India, and then permanently to Madras. When the first branch of our Society, the British T. S., was founded in London, the English Spiritualists came out in arms against us, as the Americans had done; and the French Spiritists followed suit.

ENQ. But why should the clergy be hostile to you, when, after all, the main tendency of the Theosophical doctrines is opposed to Materialism, the great enemy of all forms of religion in our day?

THEO. The Clergy opposed us on the general principle that "He who is not with me is against me." Since Theosophy does not agree with any one Sect or Creed, it is considered the enemy of all alike, because it teaches that they are all, more or less, mistaken. The missionaries in India hated and tried to crush us because they saw the flower of the educated Indian youth and the Brahmins, who are almost inaccessible to them, joining the Society in large numbers. And yet, apart from this general class hatred, the T. S. counts in its ranks many clergymen, and even one or two bishops.

ENQ. And what led the S. P. R.* to take the field against you? You were both pursuing the same line of study, in some respects, and several of the Psychic Researchers belonged to your society.

THEO. First of all we were very good friends with the leaders of the S.P.R.; but when the attack on the phenomena appeared in the *Christian College Magazine,* the S. P. R. found that they had compromised themselves by publishing in their *Proceedings* too many of the phenomena which had occurred in connection with the T. S. Their ambition is to pose as an *authoritative* and *strictly scientific* body; so that they had to choose between retaining that position by throwing overboard the T. S. and even trying to destroy it, and seeing themselves merged with the "credulous" Theosophists and Spiritualists. There was no way for them out of it, no two choices, and they chose to throw us overboard. It was a matter of dire necessity for them. But so hard pressed were they to find any apparently reasonable motive for the life of devotion and ceaseless labour led by the two Founders, and for the complete absence of any pecuniary profit or other advantage to them, that our enemies were obliged to resort to the thrice-absurd, eminently ridiculous, and now famous "Russian spy theory," to explain this devotion. After the first shock of this attack, the T.S doubled and tripled its numbers, but this bad impression produced still remains.

ENQ. Before we change the subject, let us have the whole truth on this one. Now, some writers have called your teachings "immoral and pernicious"; others, on the ground that many so-called "authorities" and Orientalists find in the Indian religions nothing but sex-worship in its many forms, accuse you of teaching nothing better than Phallic worship. They say that since modern Theosophy is so closely allied with Eastern, and particularly Indian, thought, it cannot be free from this

---

* [Society for Psychical Research]

taint. Occasionally, even, they go so far as to accuse European Theosophists of reviving the practices connected with this cult. How about this?

THEO. I have heard and read about this before; and I answer that no more utterly baseless and lying calumny has ever been invented and circulated. "Silly people can see but silly dreams," says a Russian proverb. It makes one's blood boil to hear such vile accusations made without the slightest foundation, and on the strength of mere inferences. Ask the hundreds of honourable English men and women who have been members of the Theosophical Society for years whether an *immoral* precept or a *pernicious* doctrine was ever taught to them. Such ceaseless and malicious misrepresentations of our teachings and beliefs is really disgraceful.

ENQ. But you cannot deny that the Phallic element *does* exist in the religions of the East?

THEO. Nor do I deny it; only I maintain that this proves no more than does its presence in Christianity, the religion of the West. Read Hargrave Jenning's *The Rosicrucians,* if you would assure yourself of it. In the East, the Phallic symbolism is, perhaps, more crude, because more true to nature, or, I would rather say, more *naïve* and sincere than in the West. But it is not more licentious, nor does it suggest to the Oriental mind the same gross and coarse ideas as to the Western, with, perhaps, one or two exceptions.

But you will find the whole subject dealt with at length in *The Secret Doctrine,* to which I must again refer you for detailed explanations. To conclude, the very soul of Theosophy is dead against Phallic worship; and its occult or esoteric section more so even than the exoteric teachings. There never was a more lying statement made than the above.

XIV

THE "THEOSOPHICAL MAHATMAS"

ARE THEY "SPIRITS OF LIGHT" OR "GOBLINS DAMN'D"?

ENQ. Who are they, finally, those whom you call your "Masters"?

THEO. In the first place they are *living men,* born as we are born, and doomed to die like every other mortal.

ENQ. But what does the word "Mahatma" really mean?

THEO. Simply a "great soul," great through moral elevation and intellectual attainment. If the title of great is given to a drunken soldier like Alexander, why should we not call those "Great" who have achieved far greater conquests in Nature's secrets than Alexander ever did on the field of battle? Besides, the term is an Indian and a very old word.

ENQ. And why do you call them "Masters"?

THEO. We call them "Masters" because they are our teachers; and because from them we have derived all the Theosophical truths, however inadequately some of us may have expressed, and others understood, them. They are men of great learning, whom we term Initiates, and still greater holiness of life. They are not ascetics in the ordinary sense, though they certainly remain apart from the turmoil and strife of your western world.

ENQ. But is it not selfish thus to isolate themselves?

THEO. Where is the selfishness? Does not the fate of the Theosophical Society sufficiently prove that the world is neither ready to recognize them nor to profit by their teaching? They isolate themselves only from the West. In their own country they go about as publicly as other people do.

ENQ. Don't you ascribe to them supernatural powers?

THEO. We believe in nothing supernatural, as I have told you already. The powers which they exercise are simply the development of potencies lying latent in every man and woman, and the existence of which even official science begins to recognize.

ENQ. Is it true that these men *inspire* some of your writers, and that many, if not all, of your Theosophical works were written under their dictation?

THEO. Some have. There are passages entirely dictated by them and *verbatim,* but in most cases they only inspire the ideas and leave the literary form to the writers.

ENQ. But this in itself is miraculous; is, in fact, a *miracle.* How can they do it?

THEO. My dear Sir, you are labouring under a great mistake, and it is science itself that will refute your arguments at no distant day. Why should it be a "miracle," as you call it? A miracle is supposed to mean some operation which is supernatural, whereas there is really nothing above or beyond NATURE and Nature's laws. When two minds are sympathetically related, and the instruments through which they function are tuned to respond magnetically and electrically to one another, there is nothing which will prevent the transmission of thoughts from one to the other, at will; for since the mind is not of a tangible nature, that distance can divide it from the subject of its contemplation, it follows that the only difference that can exist between two minds is a difference of STATE. So if this latter hindrance is overcome, where is the "miracle" of *thought transference,* at whatever distance?

ENQ. Tell me, have the Adepts inspired or dictated to many of your Theosophists?

THEO. No, on the contrary, to very few. Such operations require special conditions. An unscrupulous but skilled Adept of the Black Brotherhood* ("Brothers of the Shadow," and Dugpas, we call them) has far fewer difficulties to labour under. For, having no laws of the Spiritual kind to trammel his actions, such a Dugpa "sorcerer" will most unceremoniously obtain control over any mind, and subject it entirely to his evil powers. But our masters will never do that. They have no right, except by falling into Black Magic, to obtain full mastery over anyone's immortal Ego, and can therefore act only on the physical and psychic nature of the subject, leaving thereby the free will of the latter wholly undisturbed. Hence, unless a person has been brought into psychic relationship with the Masters, and is assisted by virtue of his full faith in, and devotion to, his Teachers, the latter, whenever transmitting their thoughts to one with whom these conditions are not fulfilled, experience great difficulty in penetrating into the cloudy chaos of that person's sphere. But this is no place to treat of a subject of this nature. Suffice it to say, that if the power exists, then there are Intelligences (embodied or disembodied) which guide this power, and living conscious instruments through whom it is transmitted and by whom it is received. We have only to beware of *black* magic.

ENQ. But what do you really mean by "black magic"?

THEO. Simply *abuse of psychic powers,* or of any *secret of nature;* the fact of applying to selfish and sinful ends

---

* [The use of the term "Black" has no relation to skin color. — Ed.]

the powers of Occultism. A hypnotizer, who, taking advantage of his powers of "suggestion," forces a subject to steal or murder, would be called a *black magician* by us.

ENQ. But if the Masters exist, why don't they come out before all men and refute once for all the many charges which are made against Mme. Blavatsky and the Society?

THEO. What charges?

ENQ. That *they* do not exist, and that she has invented them. That they are men of straw, "Mahatmas of muslin and bladders." Does not all this injure her reputation?

THEO. In what way can such an accusation injure her in reality? Did she ever make money on their presumed existence, or derive benefit, or fame, therefrom? I answer that she has gained only insults, abuse, and calumnies, which would have been very painful had she not learned long ago to remain perfectly indifferent to such false charges. For what does it amount to, after all? Why, to an *implied compliment,* which, if the fools, her accusers, were not carried away by their blind hatred, they would have thought twice before uttering. To say that she has invented the Masters comes to this: She must have invented every bit of philosophy that has ever been given out in Theosophical literature. She must be the author of the letters from which *Esoteric Buddhism* was written; the sole inventor of every tenet found in *The Secret Doctrine,* which, if the world were just, would be recognized as supplying many of the missing links of science, as will be discovered a hundred years hence. By saying what they do, they are also giving her the credit of being far cleverer than the hundreds of men (many *very* clever and not a few scientific men), who believe in what she says — inasmuch as she must have fooled them all! If they speak the truth, then she must be several Mahatmas rolled into one like a nest of Chinese boxes; since among the so-called "Mahatma letters" are many in totally different and distinct styles, all of which her accusers declare that she has written.

ENQ. But, of course, these Masters *do* exist?

THEO. We affirm *they* do. Many people, even some Theosophists and ex-Theosophists, say that they have never had any proof of their existence. Very well; then Mme. Blavatsky replies with this alternative: — If she has invented them, then she has also invented their philosophy and the practical knowledge which some few have acquired; and if so, what does it matter whether they do exist or not, since she herself is here, and *her own existence,* at any rate, can hardly be denied? If the knowledge supposed to have been imparted by them is good intrinsically, and it is accepted as such by many persons of more than average intelligence, why should there be such a *hullabaloo* made over that question? The fact of her being an impostor *has never been proved,* and will always remain *sub judice;* whereas it is a certain and undeniable fact that, by whomsoever invented, the philosophy preached by the "Masters" is one of the grandest and most beneficent philosophies once it is properly understood.

ENQ. But if you have such wise and good men to guide the Society, how is it that so many mistakes have been made?

THEO. The Masters do *not* guide the Society, not even the Founders; and no one has ever asserted that they did: they only watch over, and protect it. This is amply proved by the fact that no mistakes have been able to cripple it, and no scandals from within, nor the most damaging attacks from without, have been able to overthrow it. The Masters look at the future, not at the present, and every mistake is so much more accumulated wisdom for days to come. That other "Master" who sent the man with the five talents did not tell him how to double them, nor did he prevent the foolish servant from burying his one talent in the earth. Each must acquire wisdom by his own experience and merits.

THE ABUSE OF SACRED NAMES AND TERMS

ENQ. Then, what I have heard, namely, that many of your Theosophical writers claim to have been inspired by these Masters, or to have seen and conversed with them, is not true?

THEO. It may or it may not be true. How can I tell? The burden of proof rests with them. Some of them, a few — very few, indeed — have distinctly either *lied* or were hallucinated when boasting of such inspiration; others were truly inspired by great Adepts. The tree is known by its fruits; and as all Theosophists have to be judged by their deeds and not by what they write or say, so *all* Theosophical books must be accepted on their merits, and not according to any claim to authority which they may put forward.

ENQ. But would Mme. Blavatsky apply this to her own works — *The Secret Doctrine,* for instance?

THEO. Certainly; she says expressly in the PREFACE that she gives out the doctrines that she has learnt from the Masters, but claims no inspiration whatever for what she has lately written. As for our best Theosophists, they would also in this case far rather that the names of the Masters had never been mixed up with our books in any way. Great are the desecrations to which the names of two of the Masters have been subjected. There is hardly a medium who has not claimed to have seen them. Every bogus swindling Society, for commercial purposes, now claims to be guided and directed by "Masters," often supposed to be far higher than ours! Many and heavy are the sins of those who advanced these claims, prompted either by desire for lucre, vanity, or irresponsible mediumship. Many persons have been plundered of their money by such societies, which offer to sell the secrets of power, knowledge, and spiritual truth for worthless gold. Worst of all, the sacred names of Occultism and the holy keepers thereof have been dragged in this filthy mire, polluted by being associated with sordid motives and immoral practices, while thousands of men have been held back from the path of truth and light through the discredit and evil report which such shams, swindles, and frauds have brought upon the whole subject.

ENQ. The names certainly do occur very frequently nowadays, and I never remember hearing of such persons as "Masters" till quite recently.

THEO. It is so; and had we acted on the wise principle of silence, instead of rushing into notoriety and publishing all we knew and heard, such desecration would never have occurred. We Theosophists were, unfortunately, the first to talk of these things, to make the fact of the existence in the East of "Adepts" and "Masters" and Occult knowledge known; and now the name has become common property. It is on us, now, that the Karma, the consequences of the resulting desecration of holy names and things, has fallen. All that you now find about such matters in current literature — and there is not a little of it — all is to be traced back to the impulse given in this direction by the Theosophical Society and its Founders. But it is useless to grieve over what is done, and we can only suffer in the hope that our indiscretions may have made it a little easier for others to find the way to these Masters, whose names are now everywhere taken in vain, and under cover of which so many iniquities have already been perpetrated.

CONCLUSION

THE FUTURE OF THE THEOSOPHICAL SOCIETY

ENQ. Tell me, what do you expect for Theosophy in the future?

THEO. If you speak of THEOSOPHY, I answer that, as it has existed eternally throughout the endless cycles upon cycles of the Past, so it will ever exist throughout the infinitudes of the Future, because Theosophy is synonymous with EVERLASTING TRUTH.

ENQ. Pardon me; I meant to ask you rather about the prospects of the Theosophical Society.

THEO. Its future will depend almost entirely upon the degree of selflessness, earnestness, devotion, and last, but not least, on the amount of knowledge and wisdom possessed by those members, on whom it will fall to carry on the work, and to direct the Society after the death of the Founders.

ENQ. I quite see the importance of their being selfless and devoted, but I do not quite grasp how their *knowledge* can be as vital a factor in the question as these other qualities. Surely the literature which already exists, and to which constant additions are still being made, ought to be sufficient?

THEO. I do not refer to technical knowledge of the esoteric doctrine, though that is most important; I spoke rather of the great need which our successors in the guidance of the Society will have of unbiased and clear judgement. Every such attempt as the Theosophical Society has hitherto ended in failure, because, sooner or later, it has degenerated into a sect, set up hard and fast dogmas of its own, and so lost by imperceptible degrees that vitality which living truth alone can impart.

ENQ. But if this danger be averted?

THEO. Then the Society will live on into and through the twentieth century. It will gradually leaven and permeate the great mass of thinking and intelligent people with its large-minded and noble ideas of Religion, Duty, and Philanthropy. Slowly but surely it will burst asunder the iron fetters of creeds and dogmas, of social and caste prejudices; it will break down racial and national antipathies and barriers, and will open the way to the practical realization of the Brotherhood of all men. Through its teaching, through the philosophy which it has rendered accessible and intelligible to the modern mind, the West will learn to understand and appreciate the East at its true value. Further, the development of the psychic powers and faculties will proceed healthily and normally. Mankind will be saved from the terrible dangers, both mental and bodily, which are inevitable when that unfolding takes place, as it threatens to do, in a hotbed of selfishness and all evil passions. Man's mental and psychic growth will proceed in harmony with his moral improvement, while his material surroundings will reflect the peace and fraternal goodwill which will reign in his mind, instead of the discord and strife which is everywhere apparent around us today.

ENQ. A truly delightful picture! But tell me, do you really expect all this to be accomplished in one short century?

THEO. Scarcely. But I must tell you that during the last quarter of every hundred years an attempt is made by those "Masters," of whom I have spoken, to help on the spiritual progress of Humanity in a marked and definite way. Towards the close of each century you will invariably find that an outpouring or upheaval of spirituality — or call it mysticism if you prefer — has taken place. Some one or more persons have appeared in the world as their agents, and a greater or less amount of occult knowledge and teaching has been given out. If you care to do so, you can trace these movements back, century by century, as far as our detailed historical records extend.

ENQ. But how does this bear on the future of the Theosophical Society?

THEO. If the present attempt, in the form of our Society, succeeds better than its predecessors have done, then it will be in existence as an organized, living and healthy body when the time comes for the effort of the twentieth century. The general condition of men's minds and hearts will have been improved and purified by the spread of its teachings, and, as I have said, their prejudices and dogmatic illusions will have been, to some extent at least, removed. Not only so, but besides a large and accessible literature ready to men's hands, the next impulse will find a numerous and *united* body of people ready to welcome the new torch-bearer of Truth. He will find the minds of men prepared for his message, a language ready for him in which to clothe the new truths he brings, an organization awaiting his arrival, which will remove the merely mechanical, material obstacles and difficulties from his path. Think how much one, to whom such an opportunity is given, could accomplish. Consider all this, and then tell me whether I am too sanguine when I say that if the Theosophical Society survives and lives true to its mission, to its original impulses through the next hundred years — tell me, I say, if I go too far in asserting that earth will be a heaven in the twenty-first century in comparison with what it is now!

FINIS.

INDEX